Punishments for North Carolina Crimes and Motor Vehicle Offenses

Punishments for North Carolina Crimes and Motor Vehicle Offenses

by

John Rubin

and

Ben F. Loeb, Jr.

1999

Includes legislative changes enacted through the end of the 1998 session of the North Carolina General Assembly

INSTITUTE *of* GOVERNMENT
The University of North Carolina at Chapel Hill

The Institute of Government of The University of North Carolina at Chapel Hill is devoted to teaching, research, and consultation in state and local government.

Since 1931 the Institute has conducted schools and short courses for city, county, and state officials. Through monographs, guidebooks, bulletins, and periodicals, the research findings of the Institute are made available to public officials throughout the state.

Each day that the General Assembly is in session, the Institute's *Daily Bulletin* reports on the Assembly's activities for members of the legislature and other state and local officials who need to follow the course of legislation.

Over the years the Institute has served as the research agency for numerous study commissions of the state and local governments.

The University of North Carolina at Chapel Hill
♾ This publication is printed on permanent, acid-free paper in compliance with the North Carolina General Statutes.

Printed in the United States of America

ISBN 1-56011-359-6

♻ Printed on recycled paper.

Summary of Contents

Preface

In 1995 we decided to publish in one volume two earlier Institute of Government publications—the *Punishment Chart for North Carolina Crimes* and the *Punishment Chart for Motor Vehicle Offenses in North Carolina.* Because those involved in the court system must often consult both criminal and motor vehicle law, we thought that a single publication would be a more convenient reference tool. In light of the positive response to the 1995 edition, we have again combined the two punishment charts into a single volume, which represents the Institute of Government's ninth compilation of criminal offenses, motor vehicle violations, and punishments in North Carolina.

The "Punishment Chart for North Carolina Crimes," which appears in Part 1 of the book, was prepared by John Rubin. The "Punishment Chart for North Carolina Motor Vehicle Offenses," which appears in Part 2, was prepared by Ben F. Loeb, Jr. Each part stands on its own, with a detailed table of contents, a brief introduction on using the chart, the chart itself, and an index. The information is current through the close of the 1998 session of the General Assembly.

The book also contains an introduction to structured sentencing, which with few exceptions applies to all offenses committed on or after October 1, 1994. Although the punishment charts give the offense class for each felony and misdemeanor they list, knowledge of the class of offense by itself is insufficient to determine a person's sentence under structured sentencing. The introductory section therefore complements the charts by describing how structured sentencing works. Also included in the introduction are several tables necessary to determine the possible sentence a person may receive.

Producing a book of this kind is a painstaking process, and several people deserve thanks: Andrew Schopler, who assisted us with the legal research; Elaine Welch, who entered the information we gathered; Robert Farb, who read and commented on earlier drafts; Melissa Twomey, who drew the task of editing the book; and Michael Brady, who laid out and designed the final product.

We welcome comments about the book's scope, organization, and content. Comments may be sent to either of us at the Institute of Government, CB# 3330, Knapp Building, The University of North Carolina at Chapel Hill, Chapel Hill, North Carolina 27599-3330. John Rubin can be reached by telephone at (919) 962-2498 or by e-mail at **rubin@iogmail.iog.unc.edu**. Ben Loeb can be reached at (919) 966-4248 or at **loeb@iogmail.iog.unc.edu**.

John Rubin
Ben F. Loeb, Jr.

Chapel Hill
Spring 1999

Introduction
Structured Sentencing and Related Laws

Introduction
Structured Sentencing and Related Laws

Structured sentencing took effect October 1, 1994, replacing the Fair Sentencing Act, which had governed criminal sentencing in North Carolina since July 1, 1981. Structured sentencing applies to most misdemeanors and felonies committed on or after October 1, 1994.[1] The only misdemeanors not subject to structured sentencing are impaired driving under Chapter 20, Section 138.1, of the North Carolina General Statutes [hereinafter G.S.]; commercial impaired driving under G.S. 20-138.2;[2] a second or subsequent conviction of a zero tolerance offense under G.S. 20-138.3A (commercial drivers) or G.S. 20-138.3B (school bus and child care vehicle drivers);[3] and failing to comply with health control measures under G.S. 130A-25. Also exempt from structured sentencing are felonies resulting in a conviction as a violent habitual felon under G.S. 14-7.7 through -7.12. *See generally* G.S. 15A-1340.10 (noting exceptions to structured sentencing).

This chapter describes how a sentence is determined under structured sentencing. It reviews the pertinent structured sentencing statutes, which have been amended by the General Assembly each year since their adoption, and notes the key appellate decisions interpreting them. Also discussed are other sentencing provisions, such as restitution requirements, that may bear on a defendant's sentence. Readers interested in a fuller discussion of structured sentencing and sentencing in general should consult Stevens H. Clarke, *Law of Sentencing, Probation, and Parole in North Carolina* (Institute of Government, 2d ed. 1997 & Supp.), *Administration of Justice Bulletin* 99/01 (Jan. 1999) (updating *Law of Sentencing*); *North Carolina Sentencing and Policy Advisory Commission, Structured Sentencing for Felonies: Training and Reference Manual* (1998); and *North Carolina Sentencing and Policy Advisory Commission, Structured Sentencing for Misdemeanors: Training and Reference Manual* (1998).

Felonies

The centerpiece of structured sentencing for felonies is the statutory table of punishments in G.S. 15A-1340.17(c), commonly referred to as the sentencing grid. It is included as Table 1 at the end of this chapter. Other tables necessary to determine the appropriate sentence for a felony are also included in this chapter.

---

1. If an offense began before the effective date of structured sentencing but ended afterward, it also may be subject to structured sentencing. *See* State v. Mullaney, 129 N.C. App. 506, 500 S.E.2d 112 (1998).

2. For offenses committed on or after Oct. 1, 1994, and before Dec. 1, 1998, this offense was subject to structured sentencing.

3. G.S. 20-138.3A and -138.3B apply only to offenses committed on or after Dec. 1, 1998.

A sentencing court essentially must take seven steps to determine the appropriate sentence for felonies. These steps (with the appropriate sources to consult) are as follows:

1. Determine the offense class for each felony conviction (punishment charts).
2. Determine the prior record level for the defendant (Tables 3a and b).
3. Consider aggravating and mitigating factors (Tables 4a and b).
4. Select a minimum sentence from the applicable minimum sentence range (Table 1).
5. Determine the maximum sentence (Tables 2a and b).
6. Determine the sentence disposition (active, intermediate, or community) (Table 1).
7. Consider the appropriateness of restitution (Table 6).

Each of these steps is summarized below. The main exceptions are also noted below, under the heading "Special Provisions for Felonies."

Offense Class for Felonies

Generally

The first step in determining the appropriate sentence for a felony is to identify the class of the felony. There are ten classes of felonies under structured sentencing (A, B1, B2, C, D, E, F, G, H, and I).[4] For each felony listed in the punishment charts in this book, the class of the offense is indicated. For example, a violation of G.S. 14-32(c) (assault with deadly weapon with intent to kill) is a Class E felony. A violation of G.S. 20-138.5 (habitual impaired driving) is a Class F felony.

Attempt, Conspiracy, Solicitation, and Accessory after the Fact

Unless a different classification is stated in the statute governing the offense, *conspiracy* or *attempt* to commit a felony is punishable one class lower than the felony the defendant conspired or attempted to commit. *See* G.S. 14-2.4(a) (conspiracy), -2.5 (attempt). For example, pursuant to this rule, attempted common-law robbery is a Class H felony, which is one class lower than the classification of common-law robbery, a Class G felony under G.S. 14-87.1. Attempted armed robbery, however, is punishable as armed robbery, a Class D felony, because the statute governing armed robbery, G.S. 14-87, so provides.[5]

Similarly, unless a different classification is stated, *solicitation* to commit a felony or *accessory after the fact* to a felony is punishable two classes lower than the completed offense. *See* G.S. 14-2.6(a) (solicitation) and -7 (accessory after the fact).[6]

Prior Record Level for Felonies

The second step is to determine the defendant's prior record level. A defendant is assigned to one of six prior record levels (I through VI) based on the number of points he or she receives under structured sentencing. For example, a defendant with 5 to 8 points is in prior record level III. The six prior record levels, and the point

---

4. Class J felonies, established by the Fair Sentencing Act, were eliminated with the adoption of structured sentencing, and the offenses in that class were reclassified.

5. Unless a different classification is stated, attempt or conspiracy to commit a Class A or B1 felony is a Class B2 felony, attempt or conspiracy to commit a Class B2 felony is a Class C felony, and conspiracy to commit a Class I felony is a Class 1 misdemeanor (and therefore subject to misdemeanor sentencing rules).

6. Unless a different classification is stated, solicitation to commit a Class A or B1 felony is a Class C felony, solicitation to commit a Class B2 felony is a Class D felony, solicitation to commit a Class H felony is a Class 1 misdemeanor (subject to misdemeanor sentencing rules), and solicitation to commit a Class I felony is a Class 2 misdemeanor (also subject to misdemeanor sentencing rules). The same scheme applies to accessory after the fact to a felony. For offenses committed on or after Oct. 1, 1994, and before Dec. 1, 1997, accessory after the fact to a felony was a Class H felony.

ranges for each level, are indicated in Tables 3a and b at the end of this chapter. A defendant is assigned points in one of three ways, discussed below.

Prior Convictions

If a defendant has any prior convictions, points are assigned to each conviction based on the offense class of the conviction. For example, a prior conviction for a Class H felony carries 2 points. The point values for each offense class are indicated in Table 3a. Proof of prior convictions is as provided in G.S. 15A-1340.14(f). *See also* G.S. 15A-1340.11(7) (definition of final conviction); *State v. Rich,* 130 N.C. App. 113, 502 S.E.2d 49 (1998) (Division of Criminal Information printout admissible to prove prior conviction if it contains sufficient identifying information with respect to defendant). In calculating prior conviction points, the following structured sentencing rules must be kept in mind.

Prior misdemeanors. For purposes of felony sentencing, prior convictions for Class 2 and 3 misdemeanors do not count; nor do misdemeanors of any class under Chapter 20 of the General Statutes except the following, which carry 1 point:

- misdemeanor death by vehicle under G.S. 20-141.4(a2);
- regular impaired driving under G.S. 20-138.1; and
- commercial impaired driving under G.S. 20-138.2.

See G.S. 15A-1340.14(b).[7]

Current classification of prior conviction. A prior offense is classified according to the classification assigned to that offense *at the time the current offense was committed.* For example, if the defendant has a prior conviction for second-degree burglary, the points assigned to the conviction would depend on the current classification of the offense (now, Class G), *not* on the classification in effect at the time the conviction occurred. *See* G.S. 15A-1340.14(c); *see also State v. Rice,* 129 N.C. App. 715, 501 S.E.2d 665 (1998) (finding that 1972 kidnapping conviction was substantially similar to second-degree kidnapping, a Class E felony, and conviction was properly treated as that class of offense in assigning points).

Multiple prior convictions. If the defendant was convicted of more than one offense in a single superior court during one calendar week, only the conviction with the highest number of points is counted in determining prior conviction points. If the defendant was convicted of more than one offense during a single session (that is, day) of district court, only the most serious conviction is counted. *See* G.S. 15A-1340.14(d).

Convictions from other jurisdictions. Unless the prosecutor or defendant proves otherwise, a conviction from another jurisdiction is classified as a Class I felony (which carries 2 points) if that jurisdiction classifies the offense as a felony. Unless the prosecutor proves otherwise, a conviction from another jurisdiction is classified as a Class 3 misdemeanor (which carries no points for purposes of felony sentencing) if the other jurisdiction classifies the offense as a misdemeanor. *See* G.S. 15A-1340.14(e); *see also State v. Rich,* 130 N.C. App. 113, 502 S.E.2d 49 (1998) (relying on statutes from other states in determining classification of out-of-state convictions).

Time limit. The court of appeals has held that for purposes of determining prior conviction points, a prior conviction is counted regardless of how long ago it may have occurred. *See State v. Rich,* 130 N.C. App. 113, 502 S.E.2d 49 (1998) (finding that structured sentencing statutes contain no time limit on use of prior convictions for this purpose).

Same or Lesser Offenses

In addition to points for prior convictions, a defendant receives 1 point if all of the elements of the present offense are included in a prior offense. In essence, the current offense must be the same as or a lesser-included offense of a prior offense for which the defendant has been convicted. Effective for offenses committed on or

7. For sentencing for felonies committed before Dec. 1, 1997, convictions for regular or commercial impaired driving do not carry any points.

after December 1, 1997, this additional point may be counted "whether or not the prior offense or offenses were used in determining prior record level." *See* G.S. 15A-1340.14(b)(6). Thus if a defendant has a prior felony breaking and entering conviction (a Class H felony) and the current conviction is for felony breaking and entering, the defendant apparently could receive 2 points for the prior Class H felony and 1 additional point because the current offense is the same as the prior offense.

Other Points

Last, 1 point is added if, at the time the current offense was committed, the defendant was: (1) on probation (supervised or unsupervised), parole, or post-release supervision; (2) serving an active sentence of imprisonment; or (3) on escape while serving a sentence of imprisonment. *See* G.S. 15A-1340.14(b)(7).

Aggravating and Mitigating Factors for Felonies

Table 1, the sentencing grid, contains three ranges of imprisonment for felonies: presumptive, aggravated, and mitigated. To determine the range in which to sentence a defendant, the court must consider any evidence of aggravating and mitigating factors. The state has the burden of proving by a preponderance of the evidence any aggravating factors, and the defendant has the burden of proving any mitigating factors. *See* G.S. 15A-1340.16(a). The statutory aggravating factors are set forth in Table 4a. The statutory mitigating factors are set forth in Table 4b.

If the court finds that aggravating factors are present and that they outweigh any mitigating factors, it may depart from the presumptive range of imprisonment contained in Table 1 and impose a term of imprisonment from the aggravated range. Likewise, if the court finds that mitigating factors outweigh aggravating factors, it may impose a term of imprisonment from the mitigated range. If the court selects a term from the aggravated or mitigated range, the court must make written findings of the aggravating and mitigating factors. The court must make such findings regardless of whether it imposes an active or suspended term of imprisonment. *See* G.S. 15A-1340.16(b), (c); *see also State v. Caldwell*, 125 N.C. App. 161, 479 S.E.2d 282 (1997) (if court imposes term of imprisonment from presumptive range, court is not required to make findings of aggravating and mitigating factors).

Minimum Sentence for Felonies

Once the class of felony, prior record level, and aggravating and mitigating factors are determined, the court must select a minimum term of imprisonment from Table 1. To determine the minimum term, the court must locate the class of felony along the left-hand side of the grid and the prior record level along the top of the grid. The cell in which the felony class and prior record level intersect shows the possible sentences that the court may impose. The court then must determine whether to impose a term of imprisonment from the presumptive, aggravated, or mitigated ranges (expressed in months) shown in the particular cell. Last, the court must select a minimum term of imprisonment from within the applicable range. For example, if a person is convicted of a Class E felony and is in prior record level III, the presumptive range of minimum terms is from 27 to 34 months. If the court sentences the defendant in the presumptive range, it must select a single number, from 27 to 34, as the minimum term of imprisonment.

Maximum Sentence for Felonies

The judgment of the court also must contain a maximum term of imprisonment. The maximum term is set by statute based on the minimum term imposed by the court. For Class B1 through E felonies, the maximum term of imprisonment is 120 percent of the minimum term rounded to the next highest month, plus 9 months. For Class F through I felonies, the maximum term of imprisonment is 120 percent of the minimum term rounded to the next highest month. *See* G.S. 15A-1340.17(d), (e), (e1).

Minimum/maximum tables containing these calculations are shown as Tables 2a and b. Table 2a lists the maximum sentences for Class B1 through E felonies; Table 2b lists the maximums for Class F through I felonies. The numbers in each table to the left of the dash represent the minimum term of imprisonment imposed by the court, expressed in months. The numbers to the right of the dash represent the corresponding maximum term required by statute.

Sentence Disposition for Felonies

The next step is to determine the sentence disposition, prescribed in Table 1. Each cell on the grid contains a sentence disposition, signified by the letter "A," "I," or "C," or by a combination of these letters. "A" represents active punishment; "I," intermediate punishment; and "C," community punishment. The court must impose the sentence disposition indicated in the applicable cell. If a cell contains two possible dispositions (for example, I/A), the court may impose either.

Active Punishments

If the court imposes an active punishment, the minimum and maximum term of imprisonment previously determined by the court must be activated. Ordinarily if the only disposition prescribed in a particular cell is "A," the court must impose an active term of imprisonment. Upon a finding of extraordinary mitigation, however, the court may impose an intermediate punishment even when only an active punishment is prescribed. Extraordinary mitigation is authorized only if the offense is a Class B2, C, or D felony; the defendant is in prior record level I or II; *and* the offense is not a drug-trafficking offense under G.S. 90-95(h) or conspiracy to commit a drug-trafficking offense under G.S. 90-95(i). *See* G.S. 15A-1340.13(g), (h).[8]

The maximum term of imprisonment may be reduced to, but not below, the minimum term by any earned time credit, which is awarded by the Department of Correction or local jail. *See* G.S. 15A-1340.13(d); 5 NCAC 2B.0109 through 2B.0114 (regulations on earned time). A defendant who receives an active term of imprisonment for a felony is ordinarily committed to the custody of the Department of Correction; but, on request of the sheriff or board of county commissioners of a county, the court may commit the person to a local jail in that county. *See* G.S. 15A-1352(b). Whether committed to the Department of Correction or a local jail, the defendant is also entitled to credit for any time already served, which is deducted from both the minimum and maximum term of imprisonment. *See* G.S. 15-196.1.

If a defendant is convicted of a Class B1 through E felony, he or she is automatically released from prison 9 months before the end of his or her maximum term of imprisonment and is placed on post-release supervision. *See* G.S. 15A-1368.2. Thus although the maximum term of imprisonment for a Class B1 through E felony is 120% of the minimum plus 9 months, the defendant is released from prison once he or she serves 120% of the minimum. (The defendant may be released sooner if he or she has any earned time credit or credit for time served.) The period of post-release supervision is 9 months for most persons convicted of a Class B1 through E felony. But a person is subject to a far longer period of supervised release—5 years—if he or she has been convicted of a Class B1 through E felony and is required to register as a sex offender pursuant to G.S. Chapter 14, Article 27A. A person must register as a sex offender if he or she has a "reportable conviction" as defined in G.S. 14-208.6(4).[9]

The period of post-release supervision may be reduced by earned time credit. *See* G.S. 15A-1368.2(d). If the defendant violates a condition of post-release supervision—during either the shorter or longer period of supervised release—he or she may be returned to prison "up to the time remaining on his [or her] maximum imposed term." G.S. 15A-1368.3(c)(1).

---

8. For offenses committed before Dec. 1, 1995, a person convicted of conspiracy to commit a drug-trafficking offense was eligible for extraordinary mitigation.

9. Before Dec. 1, 1996, supervised release lasted a maximum of 6 months for all persons convicted of Class B1 through E felonies.

When sentencing a defendant for multiple offenses, the court may consolidate sentences, run them concurrently, or run them consecutively. If the court consolidates offenses for sentencing, the most serious offense is the controlling one—the sentence disposition and the minimum and maximum terms of imprisonment must conform to the structured sentencing rules for that offense. If the court imposes consecutive sentences, the minimum term of imprisonment is the sum of the minimum terms imposed for the offenses, and the maximum term is the sum of the maximum terms for the offenses. *See* G.S. 15A-1340.15, -1354.[10]

Intermediate Punishments

If the court imposes an intermediate punishment, it must suspend the minimum and maximum term of imprisonment and impose a period of supervised probation with at least one of the conditions described in G.S. 15A-1340.11(6). For intermediate punishments for felonies, the court is authorized to impose a period of probation from 18 to 36 months; the court may depart from this range upon finding that a longer or shorter period is necessary. The maximum initial period of probation that may be imposed is 5 years. *See* G.S. 15A-1343.2(d).

The authorized conditions for intermediate punishments are

- special probation,
- assignment to a residential program,
- house arrest with electronic monitoring,
- intensive probation,
- assignment to a day-reporting center, and
- imposition of a community penalties plan that does not include an active punishment.

Special probation involves a period of imprisonment but is still a form of intermediate punishment. Under special probation, also known as a split sentence, the court suspends the term of imprisonment, places the defendant on probation, and requires him or her to submit to a period of imprisonment as a condition of probation. The period of imprisonment pursuant to special probation may not exceed 6 months or one-fourth of the maximum term of imprisonment imposed, whichever is less. *See* G.S. 15A-1351(a). If the defendant's probation is later revoked and the original term of imprisonment is activated, the defendant must be given credit for any time served as a condition of special probation. *See State v. Farris,* 336 N.C. 552, 444 S.E.2d 182 (1994).[11]

Community Punishments

A community punishment is defined as any sentence that does not include an active or intermediate punishment. *See* G.S. 15A-1340.11(2). The court must suspend any term of imprisonment; it may not impose an active term of imprisonment or special probation requiring a period of imprisonment.

A community punishment may include unsupervised or supervised probation with any authorized condition other than one defined as an intermediate punishment. Community service and outpatient drug and

---

10. If the court imposes consecutive terms of imprisonment for more than one Class B1 through E felony, the maximum prison term for each second or subsequent Class B1 through E felony is reduced by 9 months. *See* G.S. 15A-1354(b)(1).

11. IMPACT (short for Intensive Motivational Program of Alternative Correctional Treatment but commonly known as "boot camp") was previously classified as a form of special probation and, pursuant to the rules governing special probation, the period of confinement in IMPACT could not exceed 6 months or one-half of the maximum term of imprisonment, whichever was less. Effective Dec. 1, 1998, IMPACT was reclassified as a residential treatment program, which is also an intermediate punishment. The length of a sentence to IMPACT remains the same—from 90 to 120 days—but the time limits applicable to special probation no longer appear to apply. *See* G.S. 15A-1343(b1)(2a), -1343.1. Thus a court apparently may sentence a defendant to IMPACT even though the period of confinement may be longer than one-half of the suspended term of imprisonment given the defendant. Because IMPACT is a form of confinement, however, credit may still need to be given for time served in that program should the defendant's probation be revoked and his or her sentence activated. *See* G.S. 15-196.1 (sentence must be credited with time committed to or confined in state or local correctional, mental, or other institution as result of charge); *see also* North Carolina v. Pearce, 395 U.S. 711, 89 S. Ct. 2072, 23 L. Ed. 2d 656 (1969) (punishment already exacted for offense must be fully credited against sentence).

alcohol treatment are examples of permissible conditions. For community punishments for felonies, the court is authorized to impose a period of probation from 12 to 30 months; the court may depart from this range upon finding that a longer or shorter period is necessary. *See* G.S. 15A-1343.2(d)(3). A community punishment also may consist of a fine only, without probation. *See* G.S. 15A-1340.17(b).

Fines

The court may impose a fine as part of any disposition, whether active, intermediate, or community. Unless otherwise provided by statute, the amount of the fine is in the court's discretion. *See* G.S. 15A-1340.17(b).

Restitution for Felonies

The last step is to consider the appropriateness of restitution. Effective for offenses committed on or after December 1, 1998, Article 81C of G.S. Chapter 15A (G.S. 15A-1340.24 through -1340.28) governs restitution in all criminal cases. The restitution requirements differ, however, depending on whether or not the offense is subject to the Crime Victims' Rights Act (G.S. 15A-830 through -841). The felonies subject to the Crime Victims' Rights Act are

- any Class A through E felony;
- a Class F through I felony if it is in violation of certain statutes (listed in Table 6 at the end of this chapter); and
- an attempt to commit one of the above felonies if the attempt is punishable as a felony.

The discussion below outlines the main differences between offenses subject to the Crime Victims' Rights Act and other criminal offenses in the area of restitution. The statute governing a particular offense may contain more specific restitution requirements. *See, e.g.,* G.S. 14-107 (court may require person convicted of worthless check offense to make restitution for certain service and processing charges).

For offenses subject to the Crime Victims' Rights Act, the court *must* order restitution to the victim or victim's estate. *See* G.S. 15A-1340.24(b). If probation is imposed, restitution ordered to the victim must be made a condition of probation. Even if the defendant is sentenced to active imprisonment, the court apparently must order restitution to the victim or victim's estate. If a restitution order to a victim is for more than $250, it is enforceable as a civil judgment and, in some circumstances, may be subject to immediate execution. *See* G.S. 15A-1340.28.[12]

In cases not subject to the Crime Victims' Rights Act, the court must consider whether restitution is appropriate, but the court is not required to order it. *See* G.S. 15A-1340.24(a), (c). Thus the court may make restitution a condition of probation. Apparently the court also may impose restitution as part of a sentence of active imprisonment. In cases not subject to the Crime Victims' Rights Act, however, a restitution order is not enforceable as a civil judgment. The victim or victim's estate may bring a civil suit for damages resulting from the crime [*see* G.S. 15A-1340.27(a)]; but in such a suit the amount of restitution imposed is not admissible in evidence, and the defendant has the right to contest the amount of damages claimed. *See* G.S. 1-15.1.

In both kinds of cases, if the defendant is sentenced to active imprisonment, the court also must consider whether to recommend to the Department of Correction that restitution be made from any work-release earnings. *See* G.S. 15A-1340.26(c). For Class B1 through E felonies, restitution is a mandatory condition of post-

12. The judgment is not subject to execution during appeal of the underlying conviction. If the defendant is placed on probation, the judgment ordinarily is not subject to execution until probation is terminated or revoked. *See* G.S. 15A-1340.28. If the defendant is not placed on probation and the conviction is not appealed, the judgment apparently is subject to immediate execution on the victim's request unless the court has deferred payment. *See* G.S. 15A-1340.26(b) (court may set payment date or payment schedule). Effective for offenses committed on or after July 1, 1999, the defendant is not entitled to claim statutory exemptions against execution. *See* G.S. 1C-1601(e). The defendant may claim constitutional exemptions, however. *See* N.C. CONST. art. X.

release supervision. *See* G.S. 15A-1340.24(b) (restitution must be condition of post-release supervision in cases subject to Crime Victims' Rights Act, which include all Class B1 through E felonies).

The losses and injuries for which restitution may be ordered are described in G.S. 15A-1340.25. In determining the amount of restitution, the court must have adequate proof of the injuries or losses claimed and must take into account the defendant's ability to pay. *See* G.S. 15A-1340.26. The court also may (but is not required to) order restitution to persons other than the victim or to organizations as provided in G.S. 15A-1340.27.

Special Provisions for Felonies

A number of provisions depart from the basic structured sentencing scheme for felonies. The principal exceptions are described below.

Class A and B1 Felonies

Class A felonies are punishable by death or by life without parole, regardless of the defendant's prior record level. The only Class A felony is first-degree murder under G.S. 14-17.

For offenses committed before December 1, 1998, a defendant sentenced to life without parole is entitled to seek review of the sentence by a superior court judge after serving 25 years in prison. The judge must then recommend to the governor whether the sentence should be altered or commuted. *See* G.S. 15A-1380.5. For offenses committed on or after December 1, 1998, the statute requiring this procedure is repealed. The repeal does not affect the power of the governor, under Art. III, Sec. 5(6), of the North Carolina Constitution, to grant pardons and commute sentences.

Effective for offenses committed on or after January 1, 1999, G.S. 15A-1340.16B provides for life imprisonment without parole for a Class B1 felony if the offense was committed against a person age 13 or younger, the defendant has at least one prior conviction for a Class B1 felony, and there are no mitigating factors. If one or more of these conditions is not met, the court must sentence the defendant according to the regular structured sentencing rules. The only Class B1 felonies are first-degree forcible or statutory rape (*see* G.S. 14-27.2), first-degree forcible or statutory sexual offense (*see* G.S. 14-27.4), and statutory rape or sexual offense against a person who is 13, 14, or 15 years old where the defendant is at least 6 years older than the person (*see* G.S. 14-27.7A).

Habitual Felons

A defendant found to be a habitual felon (that is, convicted of a felony for a fourth time pursuant to the procedures in G.S. 14-7.1 through -7.6) is sentenced as though convicted of a Class C felony (unless the offense is a Class A, B1, or B2 felony). For example, if a defendant is convicted of felony breaking and entering (a Class H felony) and is found to be a habitual felon, he or she is sentenced as though convicted of a Class C felony. Additional sentencing rules apply in such cases, which are discussed in the "Punishment Chart for Crimes," G.S. 14-7.1 to -7.6 and accompanying note.

Special rules also govern the calculation of the prior record level of a person found to be a habitual felon. If a prior conviction is used to establish the defendant's status as a habitual felon, the conviction may not be used to determine the defendant's prior convictions under structured sentencing. *See* G.S. 14-7.6. For example, if the defendant has three prior convictions for felony breaking and entering and those convictions are used to establish the defendant's status as a habitual felon, they may not be counted in determining prior record level.

The court of appeals has found some exceptions to this rule, however. In *State v. McRae,* 124 N.C. App. 664, 478 S.E.2d 210 (1996), the court held that if two convictions were consolidated for judgment in a prior case (ordinarily treated by structured sentencing as a single conviction), one conviction may be used to establish habitual felon status and the other conviction may be used to determine the defendant's prior convictions. In *State v. Bethea,* 122 N.C. App. 623, 471 S.E.2d 430 (1996), the court held that a defendant may receive 1 point if the current offense is the same as or a lesser offense of a prior conviction, even though the prior conviction is also used to establish habitual felon status; likewise, the court held that a defendant may receive 1 point if he or she committed the current offense while on probation for a prior conviction, even though the prior conviction is used to establish habitual felon status.

If a defendant is found to be a habitual felon and is later convicted of another felony, the question arises of how many points to assign to the earlier conviction. For example, if the defendant is convicted of felony breaking and entering, found to be a habitual felon, and later convicted of another felony, is the prior breaking and entering conviction treated as a Class H felony, which carries 2 points, or a Class C felony, which carries 6 points? In *State v. Vaughn,* 130 N.C. App. 456, 503 S.E.2d 110 (1998), *aff'd per curiam,* 350 N.C. 88, 511 S.E.2d 638 (1999), the court held that the class of the underlying offense is controlling, so 2 points would be assigned to the conviction in the above example.

Violent Habitual Felons

A defendant convicted for the third time of a violent felony within the meaning of G.S. 14-7.7 through -7.12 must be sentenced to life without parole, regardless of the defendant's prior record level. Additional sentencing rules apply in such cases, which are discussed in the "Punishment Chart for Crimes," G.S. 14-7.7 to -7.12 and accompanying note.

For offenses committed before December 1, 1998, a person found to be a violent habitual felon and sentenced to life without parole is entitled to seek review of the sentence by a superior court judge after serving 25 years in prison. This procedure and its repeal are discussed above in connection with sentencing for Class A felonies.

Habitual Impaired Driving

Effective for offenses committed on or after December 1, 1997, a defendant convicted of habitual impaired driving under G.S. 20-138.5, a Class F felony, must be sentenced to an active term of imprisonment of at least 12 months. Although structured sentencing (which applies to habitual impaired driving) sometimes allows a suspended sentence for Class F felonies, the 12-month term of imprisonment may not be suspended.

Firearm Enhancement

Subject to certain exceptions, a defendant who used, displayed, or threatened to use or display a firearm during the commission of a Class A through E felony must be sentenced to an additional 60 months imprisonment. *See* G.S. 15A-1340.16A(a); 14-2.2(a). Using a firearm in this manner is not a crime; it is instead a circumstance that results in an enhanced punishment upon conviction of the underlying felony.[13] These sections provide that the court may not suspend, or place the person on probation for, this additional sentence. G.S. 14-2.2(a) (although not G.S. 15A-1340.16A) also provides that the 60-month sentence "shall be consecutive to all other sentences imposed and shall begin at the expiration of any other sentence being served by the person."

The firearm enhancement is inapplicable if: (1) the person is not sentenced to an active term of imprisonment; (2) the evidence of the use, display, or threatened use or display of a firearm is necessary to prove an element of the underlying felony; or (3) the person did not actually possess a firearm about his or her person. *See* G.S. 15A-1340.40.16A(b), 14-2.2(b); *see also* G.S. 15A-1340.16(d) (evidence necessary to establish firearm enhancement may not be used to prove any aggravating factor).

The applicability of the second exception turns on the facts of each case, as the pertinent inquiry is whether use of a firearm is necessary to prove an element of the offense, not whether use of a firearm is an actual element of the offense. *See State v. Ruff,* 349 N.C. 213, 505 S.E.2d 579 (1998) (firearm enhancement proper for second-degree kidnapping); *State v. Brice,* 126 N.C. App. 788, 486 S.E.2d 719 (1997) (enhancement not proper

13. G.S. 15A-1340.16A and 14-2.2 leave to the sentencing judge the determination of whether the conditions for the firearm enhancement have been met. *But see generally* Jones v. United States, ___ U.S. ___, 119 S. Ct. 1215 (1999) (finding that conditions in federal carjacking statute increasing maximum penalty for offense were offense elements and had to be charged by indictment, submitted to jury, and proven beyond reasonable doubt).

for kidnapping); *State v. Smith,* 125 N.C. App. 562, 481 S.E.2d 425 (1997) (enhancement not proper for voluntary manslaughter); *State v. Evans,* 125 N.C. App. 301, 480 S.E.2d 435 (1997) (enhancement proper for first-degree kidnapping). *See also State v. Williams,* 127 N.C. App. 464, 490 S.E.2d 583 (1997) (relying on third exception, court finds that enhancement not proper for second-degree kidnapping because evidence established that object displayed was not firearm).

Drug-trafficking Offenses

Drug trafficking is punished according to a separate table of punishments, containing minimum and maximum terms of imprisonment that depart from the structured sentencing grid and do not depend on the defendant's prior record. Minimum fines also are prescribed for these offenses. The minimum and maximum terms of imprisonment for drug-trafficking offenses appear in note 195 of the "Punishment Chart for Crimes." Also discussed in that note are additional rules governing sentencing for drug-trafficking offenses. For example, the court may reduce the fine, impose a prison term less than the applicable minimum, or suspend the prison term in some circumstances. The minimum fines for drug-trafficking offenses vary with the class of offense and the amount and nature of the controlled substance, which are indicated in the body of the "Punishment Chart for Crimes," G.S. 90-95(h)(1) through -95(h)(4a).

The same mandatory minimums and exceptions apply to a conspiracy to commit a drug trafficking offense. *See* "Punishment Chart for Crimes," G.S. 90-95(i) and accompanying note. These punishments do not apply to an attempt to commit a drug-trafficking offense, however. *See* "Punishment Chart for Crimes," G.S. 90-98 and accompanying note.

Misdemeanors

The focus of structured sentencing for misdemeanors is the statutory table of punishments in G.S. 15A-1340.23(c) (Table 5 at the end of this chapter). A sentencing court essentially must take five steps to determine the appropriate sentence for a misdemeanor. These steps (with the appropriate sources to consult) are as follows:

- Determine the offense class for each misdemeanor conviction (punishment charts)
- Determine the prior conviction level for the defendant (Table 5)
- Select a sentence length from the appropriate sentence range (Table 5)
- Determine the sentence disposition (active, intermediate, or community) (Table 5)
- Consider the appropriateness of restitution (Table 6)

Offense Class for Misdemeanors

Generally

The first step in determining the appropriate sentence for a misdemeanor is to identify the class of the misdemeanor. Under the initial version of structured sentencing, there were three misdemeanor classes (1, 2, and 3). Effective for offenses committed on or after December 1, 1995, a fourth misdemeanor class (A1) was added, which now is the most serious class of misdemeanor. For each misdemeanor listed in the punishment charts in this book, the class of the offense is indicated. For example, a violation of G.S. 14-34 (assault by pointing gun) is a Class A1 misdemeanor. A violation of G.S. 20-217 (passing a stopped school bus) is a Class 2 misdemeanor.

Misdemeanors without Classification/Punishment

Some misdemeanor offenses in the General Statutes have neither a classification nor a punishment listed. Under G.S. 14-3(a), such offenses ordinarily are considered Class 1 misdemeanors. If a misdemeanor has no classification and no punishment specified, and if the offense is infamous, done in secrecy and malice, or committed with deceit and intent to defraud, it may be punished as a Class H felony. For cases discussing this punishment enhancement, see "Punishment Chart for Crimes," G.S. 14-3(b) and accompanying note.

Some misdemeanor offenses have a punishment but no classification listed. Under G.S. 14-3(a), these offenses are classified as follows: as Class 1 misdemeanors if punishable by more than 6 months imprisonment; as Class 2 misdemeanors if punishable by more than 30 days but not more than 6 months imprisonment; and as Class 3 misdemeanors if punishable by imprisonment of 30 days or less or by a fine only.

Some misdemeanors are common-law offenses and do not appear at all in the General Statutes—for example, common-law obstruction of justice. By operation of G.S. 14-3(a), these offenses ordinarily are treated as Class 1 misdemeanors because they have no classification or punishment. If infamous, done in secrecy and malice, or committed with deceit and intent to defraud, a common-law misdemeanor may be punished as a Class H felony by virtue of G.S. 14-3(b).

Attempt, Conspiracy, Solicitation, and Accessory after the Fact

Unless a different classification is stated in the statute governing the offense, *conspiracy* or *attempt* to commit a misdemeanor is punishable one class lower than the misdemeanor the defendant conspired or attempted to commit. Unless a different classification is stated, conspiracy or attempt to commit a Class I felony is a Class 1 misdemeanor, and thus is subject to misdemeanor sentencing rules, and conspiracy or attempt to commit a Class 3 misdemeanor is a Class 3 misdemeanor. *See* G.S. 14-2.4 (conspiracy), -2.5 (attempt).

Unless a different classification is stated, solicitation to commit a Class H felony is a Class 1 misdemeanor, solicitation to commit a Class I felony is a Class 2 misdemeanor, and solicitation to commit a misdemeanor is a Class 3 misdemeanor. *See* G.S. 14-2.6. Unless a different classification is stated, the same punishment scheme applies to *accessory after the fact* to a Class H or Class I felony. *See* G.S. 14-7 (offense of accessory after fact to felony).[14] In the absence of a statute providing otherwise, a person apparently may not be convicted of being an accessory after the fact to a misdemeanor. *See* Wayne R. LaFave & Austin W. Scott, Jr., *Substantive Criminal Law* § 6.9(a), at 167 (1986); Rollin M. Perkins & Ronald N. Boyce, *Criminal Law* 726 (3d ed. 1982).

Prior Conviction Level for Misdemeanors

The second step is to determine the defendant's prior conviction level. A defendant is assigned to one of three prior conviction levels (I through III) based on the total number of prior felony and misdemeanor convictions. The three prior conviction levels and the number of convictions applicable to each level are indicated in Table 5.

Each conviction, whether for a felony or a misdemeanor (including misdemeanors under Chapter 20), counts as one conviction. If the defendant was convicted of more than one offense in a single week of superior court, only one of the convictions counts. If the defendant was convicted of more than one offense during a single session (that is, day) of district court, only one of the convictions counts. Infractions do not count. *See* G.S. 15A-1340.21.

A prior offense may be counted as a conviction only if the offense is classified as a felony or misdemeanor at the time the defendant committed the current offense. For example, if an offense has been changed from a misdemeanor to an infraction (for example, driving 50 mph in a 35 mph zone), a prior conviction for that offense would not count in misdemeanor sentencing. *See* G.S. 15A-1340.21(b).

Sentence Length for Misdemeanors

Once the class of misdemeanor and prior conviction level are determined, the court must determine the length of any term of imprisonment. (If the court selects a community punishment as the sentence disposition, discussed below, it may impose a judgment consisting of a fine only; in those circumstances, it would be unnecessary for the court to specify any term of imprisonment.) To determine the length of any term of imprisonment,

14. For offenses committted on or after Oct. 1, 1994, and before Dec. 1, 1997, accessory after the fact to a felony was a Class H felony.

the court must locate the class of misdemeanor along the left-hand side of Table 5 and the prior conviction level along the top of Table 5. The cell in which the misdemeanor class and prior conviction level intersect shows the possible terms of imprisonment (expressed in days) that the court may impose. The court must select a single term of imprisonment from the range shown in the applicable cell; there is no minimum and maximum term of imprisonment, as in felony sentencing.

Sentence Disposition for Misdemeanors

The next step is to determine the sentence disposition, which is prescribed in Table 5. Each cell in Table 5 contains a sentence disposition, signified by the letter "A," "I," or "C," or by a combination of these letters. "A" represents active punishment; "I," intermediate punishment; "C," community punishment. The court must impose the sentence disposition indicated in the applicable cell. If a cell authorizes more than one possible disposition (for example, C/I/A), the court may impose any of the indicated dispositions.

Active Punishments

If the court imposes an active punishment, the term of imprisonment previously determined by the court must be activated. A defendant's term of imprisonment may be reduced by earned time credit of up to 4 days per month of incarceration (awarded by the Department of Correction or local jail). *See* G.S. 15A-1340.20(d).[15] The defendant also must receive credit for time already served. *See* G.S. 15-196.1.

A defendant who receives an active term of imprisonment of 90 days or less for a misdemeanor ordinarily must be committed to a local jail. If the term of imprisonment is for more than 90 days, the court may commit the defendant to either the Department of Correction or a local jail. *See* G.S. 15A-1352(a).

The court may sentence a defendant to "time served"—that is, a term of imprisonment equal to the amount of time the defendant spent in jail before trial. A sentence of time served is technically a form of active punishment because it involves a term of imprisonment; however, the court may impose a sentence of time served for *any* misdemeanor, regardless of whether an active punishment would otherwise be authorized for that class of misdemeanor and prior conviction level. *See* G.S. 15A-1340.20(c1).

When sentencing a defendant for multiple misdemeanors, the court may consolidate sentences, run them concurrently, and subject to certain limitations impose consecutive sentences. If the court consolidates offenses for sentencing, the most serious offense is the controlling one—the sentence disposition and the term of imprisonment must conform to the structured sentencing rules for that offense.

If the court imposes consecutive sentences for misdemeanors, the length of the term of imprisonment (active or suspended) may not exceed twice the longest term of imprisonment authorized for the most serious misdemeanor conviction. Consecutive sentences may not be imposed if all of the convictions are for Class 3 misdemeanors. *See* G.S. 15A-1340.22, -1354(a).

For example, assume the defendant is convicted of three misdemeanors—Class 1, 2, and 3—and is in prior conviction level III. If the court elects to impose consecutive sentences, the cumulative term of imprisonment may not exceed 240 days, which is twice the longest possible term for a Class 1 misdemeanor, the most serious misdemeanor conviction in this example. However, the longest term of imprisonment that actually could be imposed in this example would be 200 days—120 days for the Class 1 misdemeanor, 60 days for the Class 2 misdemeanor, and 20 days for the Class 3 misdemeanor.

Intermediate Punishments

If the court imposes an intermediate punishment, the court must suspend the term of imprisonment and impose a period of supervised probation with at least one of the conditions described in G.S. 15A-1340.11(6). For intermediate punishments for misdemeanors, the court is authorized to impose a period of probation ranging from 12 to 24 months; the court may depart from this range upon finding that a longer or shorter period

15. A defendant committed to a local jail also may receive work credit under G.S. 162-60, but the total amount of earned time and work credit may not exceed 4 days per month. *See* G.S. 15A-1340.20(d).

is necessary. The maximum initial period of probation that may be imposed is 5 years. *See* G.S. 15A-1343.2(d).

The permissible intermediate punishments for misdemeanors are the same as for felonies (special probation, assignment to a residential program, house arrest with electronic monitoring, intensive probation, assignment to a day-reporting center, or imposition of a community penalties plan). If the court imposes special probation as an intermediate punishment, the period of imprisonment is limited in the same manner as for felonies—it may not exceed 6 months or one-fourth of the maximum term of imprisonment imposed, whichever is less. *See* G.S. 15A-1351(a). If the defendant's probation is later revoked and the original term of imprisonment is activated, the defendant must be given credit for any time served as a condition of special probation. *See State v. Farris,* 336 N.C. 552, 444 S.E.2d 182 (1994).[16]

Community Punishments

A community punishment is defined as any sentence that does not include an active or intermediate punishment. *See* G.S. 15A-1340.11(2). The court must suspend any term of imprisonment; it may not impose an active term of imprisonment or special probation requiring a period of imprisonment.

A community punishment may consist of unsupervised or supervised probation with any authorized condition other than one defined as an intermediate punishment. Community service and outpatient drug and alcohol treatment are examples of permissible conditions. For community punishments for misdemeanors, the court is authorized to impose a period of probation ranging from 6 to 18 months; the court may depart from this range upon finding that a longer or shorter period is necessary. *See* G.S. 15A-1343.2(d)(1). A community punishment also may consist of a fine only, without probation. *See* G.S. 15A-1340.23(b).

Fines

The court may impose a fine as part of any disposition, whether active, intermediate, or community. Unless otherwise provided by statute, the maximum fine for each class of misdemeanor is as indicated in Table 5. For example, although the maximum fine for a Class 3 misdemeanor is ordinarily $200, a violation of G.S. 14-118.5 (unauthorized interception of cable television service) is punishable by a fine of up to $500, while a violation of G.S. 14-140.1 (burning material without watchman) is punishable by a fine of up to $50.

Restitution for Misdemeanors

The last step is to consider the appropriateness of restitution. The restitution requirements in G.S. 15A-1340.24 through -1340.28, discussed above in connection with felonies, apply equally to misdemeanors. Thus the sentencing court must determine whether a misdemeanor is subject to the Crime Victims' Rights Act (G.S. 15A-830 through -841), which for certain offenses mandates restitution to the victim and allows enforcement of the restitution order as a civil judgment. For misdemeanors not subject to the Crime Victims' Rights Act, the court must consider the appropriateness of restitution, but the court is not required to order it.

The main difference with restitution in misdemeanor versus felony cases is that far fewer misdemeanors are subject to the Crime Victims' Rights Act. Only certain misdemeanors are covered:

- assault with a deadly weapon,
- assault inflicting serious injury,
- assault by pointing a gun,
- domestic criminal trespass, and
- stalking.

Further, the Crime Victims' Rights Act applies to the above misdemeanors only if the defendant and victim were in one of six different "personal relationships" (for example, as current or former spouses) described in G.S. 50B-1(b). Table 6 at the end of this chapter lists the offenses subject to the Crime Victims' Rights Act.

16. For a discussion of IMPACT, which was formerly classified as a form of special probation and is now classified as a residential treatment program, *see* note 11, above.

Table 1

Felony Sentence Dispositions and Minimum Terms of Imprisonment (in months)

A = active punishment I = intermediate punishment C = community punishment

Felony Offense Class	Prior Record Level I 0 Points	II 1–4 Points	III 5–8 Points	IV 9–14 Points	V 15–18 Points	VI 19+ Points	
A	Life imprisonment without parole or death						
B1	A	A	A	A	A	A	DISPOSITION
	240–300	288–360	336–420	384–480	Life without parole		Aggravated
	192–240	230–288	269–336	307–384	346–433	384–480	Presumptive
	144–192	173–230	202–269	230–307	260–346	288–384	Mitigated
B2 offense before 12/1/95	A	A	A	A	A	A	DISPOSITION
	135–169	163–204	190–238	216–270	243–304	270–338	Aggravated
	108–135	130–163	152–190	173–216	194–243	216–270	Presumptive
	81–108	98–130	114–152	130–173	146–194	162–216	Mitigated
B2 offense on or after 12/1/95	A	A	A	A	A	A	DISPOSITION
	157–196	189–237	220–276	251–313	282–353	313–392	Aggravated
	125–157	151–189	176–220	201–251	225–282	251–313	Presumptive
	94–125	114–151	132–176	151–201	169–225	188–251	Mitigated
C offense before 12/1/95	A	A	A	A	A	A	DISPOSITION
	63–79	86–108	100–125	115–144	130–162	145–181	Aggravated
	50–63	69–86	80–100	92–115	104–130	116–145	Presumptive
	38–50	52–69	60–80	69–92	78–104	87–116	Mitigated
C offense on or after 12/1/95	A	A	A	A	A	A	DISPOSITION
	73–92	100–125	116–145	133–167	151–188	168–210	Aggravated
	58–73	80–100	93–116	107–133	121–151	135–168	Presumptive
	44–58	60–80	70–93	80–107	90–121	101–135	Mitigated
D offense before 12/1/95	A	A	A	A	A	A	DISPOSITION
	55–69	66–82	89–111	101–126	115–144	126–158	Aggravated
	44–55	53–66	71–89	81–101	92–115	101–126	Presumptive
	33–44	40–53	53–71	61–81	69–92	76–101	Mitigated
D offense on or after 12/1/95	A	A	A	A	A	A	DISPOSITION
	64–80	77–95	103–129	117–146	133–167	146–183	Aggravated
	51–64	61–77	82–103	94–117	107–133	117–146	Presumptive
	38–51	46–61	61–82	71–94	80–107	88–117	Mitigated
E	I/A	I/A	A	A	A	A	DISPOSITION
	25–31	29–36	34–42	46–58	53–66	59–74	Aggravated
	20–25	23–29	27–34	37–46	42–53	47–59	Presumptive
	15–20	17–23	20–27	28–37	32–42	35–47	Mitigated
F	I/A	I/A	I/A	A	A	A	DISPOSITION
	16–20	19–24	21–26	25–31	34–42	39–49	Aggravated
	13–16	15–19	17–21	20–25	27–34	31–39	Presumptive
	10–13	11–15	13–17	15–20	20–27	23–31	Mitigated
G	I/A	I/A	I/A	I/A	A	A	DISPOSITION
	13–16	15–19	16–20	20–25	21–26	29–36	Aggravated
	10–13	12–15	13–16	16–20	17–21	23–29	Presumptive
	8–10	9–12	10–13	12–16	13–17	17–23	Mitigated
H	C/I/A*	I/A*	I/A	I/A	I/A	A	DISPOSITION
	6–8	8–10	10–12	11–14	15–19	20–25	Aggravated
	5–6	6–8	8–10	9–11	12–15	16–20	Presumptive
	4–5	4–6	6–8	7–9	9–12	12–16	Mitigated
I	C	C/I	I	I/A	I/A	I/A	DISPOSITION
	6–8	6–8	6–8	8–10	9–11	10–12	Aggravated
	4–6	4–6	5–6	6–8	7–9	8–10	Presumptive
	3–4	3–4	4–5	4–6	5–7	6–8	Mitigated

*Active punishment is authorized only if the offense occurred on or after Dec. 1, 1995.
SOURCE: G.S. 15A-1340.17(c).

Table 2a
Felony Minimum and Maximum Prison/Jail Terms
(shown in months)

Felony Classes B1, B2, C, D, and E							
15–27	56–77	97–126	138–175	179–224	220–273	261–323	302–372
16–29	57–78	98–127	139–176	180–225	221–275	262–324	303–373
17–30	58–79	99–128	140–177	181–227	222–276	263–325	304–374
18–31	59–80	100–129	141–179	182–228	223–277	264–326	305–375
19–32	60–81	101–131	142–180	183–229	224–278	265–327	306–377
20–33	61–83	102–132	143–181	184–230	225–279	266–329	307–378
21–35	62–84	103–133	144–182	185–231	226–281	267–330	308–379
22–36	63–85	104–134	145–183	186–233	227–282	268–331	309–380
23–37	64–86	105–135	146–185	187–234	228–283	269–332	310–381
24–38	65–87	106–137	147–186	188–235	229–284	270–333	311–383
25–39	66–89	107–138	148–187	189–236	230–285	271–335	312–384
26–41	67–90	108–139	149–188	190–237	231–287	272–336	313–385
27–42	68–91	109–140	150–189	191–239	232–288	273–337	314–386
28–43	69–92	110–141	151–191	192–240	233–289	274–338	315–387
29–44	70–93	111–143	152–192	193–241	234–290	275–339	316–389
30–45	71–95	112–144	153–193	194–242	235–291	276–341	317–390
31–47	72–96	113–145	154–194	195–243	236–293	277–342	318–391
32–48	73–97	114–146	155–195	196–245	237–294	278–343	319–392
33–49	74–98	115–147	156–197	197–246	238–295	279–344	320–393
34–50	75–99	116–149	157–198	198–247	239–296	280–345	321–395
35–51	76–101	117–150	158–199	199–248	240–297	281–347	322–396
36–53	77–102	118–151	159–200	200–249	241–299	282–348	323–397
37–54	78–103	119–152	160–201	201–251	242–300	283–349	324–398
38–55	79–104	120–153	161–203	202–252	243–301	284–350	325–399
39–56	80–105	121–155	162–204	203–253	244–302	285–351	326–401
40–57	81–107	122–156	163–205	204–254	245–303	286–353	327–402
41–59	82–108	123–157	164–206	205–255	246–305	287–354	328–403
42–60	83–109	124–158	165–207	206–257	247–306	288–355	329–404
43–61	84–110	125–159	166–209	207–258	248–307	289–356	330–405
44–62	85–111	126–161	167–210	208–259	249–308	290–357	331–407
45–63	86–113	127–162	168–211	209–260	250–309	291–359	332–408
46–65	87–114	128–163	169–212	210–261	251–311	292–360	333–409
47–66	88–115	129–164	170–213	211–263	252–312	293–361	334–410
48–67	89–116	130–165	171–215	212–264	253–313	294–362	335–411
49–68	90–117	131–167	172–216	213–265	254–314	295–363	336–413
50–69	91–119	132–168	173–217	214–266	255–315	296–365	337–414
51–71	92–120	133–169	174–218	215–267	256–317	297–366	338–415
52–72	93–121	134–170	175–219	216–269	257–318	298–367	339–416
53–73	94–122	135–171	176–221	217–270	258–319	299–368	340 or more*
54–74	95–123	136–173	177–222	218–271	259–320	300–369	
55–75	96–125	137–174	178–223	219–272	260–321	301–371	

*Where minimum term is 340 months or more, maximum is 120% of minimum rounded to next highest month, plus 9 months.

SOURCE: G.S. 15A-1340.17(e), (e1).

Table 2b
Felony Minimum and Maximum Prison/Jail Terms
(shown in months)

Felony Classes F, G, H, and I							
3–4	9–11	15–18	21–26	27–33	33–40	39–47	45–54
4–5	10–12	16–20	22–27	28–34	34–41	40–48	46–56
5–6	11–14	17–21	23–28	29–35	35–42	41–50	47–57
6–8	12–15	18–22	24–29	30–36	36–44	42–51	48–58
7–9	13–16	19–23	25–30	31–38	37–45	43–52	49–59
8–10	14–17	20–24	26–32	32–39	38–46	44–53	

SOURCE: G.S. 15A-1340.17(d).

Table 3a
Prior Record Points for Felonies

Prior Conviction or Other Factor	Points
Each prior Class A felony conviction	10
Each prior Class B1 felony conviction	9
Each prior Class B2, C, or D felony conviction	6
Each prior Class E, F, or G felony conviction	4
Each prior Class H or I felony conviction	2
Each prior Class A1 or 1 misdemeanor conviction (but no points for misdemeanors of any class under G.S. Ch. 20 except for misdemeanor death by vehicle and, effective for felonies committed on or after Dec. 1, 1997, regular impaired driving and commercial impaired driving)	1
All the elements of the present offense are included in a prior offense—maximum 1 point	1
Present offense was committed while offender was on probation, parole, or post-release supervision, was serving a term of imprisonment, or was on escape while serving a term of imprisonment—maximum 1 point	1

SOURCE: G.S. 15A-1340.14(b).

Table 3b
Prior Record Levels for Felonies

Prior Record Level	Total Point Score
Level I	0
Level II	1–4
Level III	5–8
Level IV	9–14
Level V	15–18
Level VI	19 or more

SOURCE: G.S. 15A-1340.14(c).

Table 4a
Aggravating Factors

1. The defendant induced others to participate in the commission of the offense or occupied a position of leadership or dominance of other participants.
2. The defendant joined with more than one other person in committing the offense and was not charged with committing a conspiracy.

2a.* The offense was committed for the benefit of, or at the direction of, any criminal street gang, with the specific intent to promote, further, or assist in any criminal conduct by gang members, and the defendant was not charged with committing a conspiracy. A 'criminal street gang' means any ongoing organization, association, or group of three or more persons, whether formal or informal, having as one of its primary activities the commission of felony or violent misdemeanor offenses, or delinquent acts that would be felonies or violent misdemeanors if committed by an adult, and having a common name or common identifying sign, colors, or symbols.

3. The offense was committed for the purpose of avoiding or preventing a lawful arrest or effecting an escape from custody.
4. The defendant was hired or paid to commit the offense.
5. The offense was committed to disrupt or hinder the lawful exercise of any governmental function or the enforcement of laws.

6.** The offense was committed against or proximately caused serious injury to a present or former law enforcement officer, employee of the Department of Correction, jailer, firefighter, emergency medical technician, ambulance attendant, justice or judge, clerk or assistant or deputy clerk of court, magistrate, prosecutor, juror, or witness against the defendant, while engaged in the performance of that person's official duties or because of the exercise of that person's official duties.

7. The offense was especially heinous, atrocious, or cruel.
8. The defendant knowingly created a great risk of death to more than one person by means of a weapon or device which would normally be hazardous to the lives of more than one person.
9. The defendant held public office at the time of the offense and the offense related to the conduct of the office.
10. The defendant was armed with or used a deadly weapon at the time of the crime.
11. The victim was very young, or very old, or mentally or physically infirm, or handicapped.
12. The defendant committed the offense while on pretrial release on another charge.
13. The defendant involved a person under the age of 16 in the commission of the crime.
14. The offense involved an attempted or actual taking of property of great monetary value or damage causing great monetary loss, or the offense involved an unusually large quantity of contraband.
15. The defendant took advantage of a position of trust or confidence to commit the offense.
16. The offense involved the sale or delivery of a controlled substance to a minor.
17. The offense for which the defendant stands convicted was committed against a victim because of the victim's race, color, religion, nationality, or country of origin.
18. The defendant does not support the defendant's family.

18a. The defendant has previously been adjudicated delinquent for an offense that would be a Class A, B1, B2, C, D or E felony if committed by an adult.

19. The serious injury inflicted upon the victim is permanent and debilitating.
20. Any other aggravating factor reasonably related to the purposes of sentencing.

*This factor applies to offenses committed on or after Dec. 1, 1997.

**Effective for offenses committed on or after Dec. 1, 1997, this factor was revised to cover offenses that "proximately caused serious injury" to the designated persons, in addition to offenses committed against such persons.

SOURCE: G.S. 15A-1340.16(d).

Table 4b
Mitigating Factors

1. The defendant committed the offense under duress, coercion, threat, or compulsion that was insufficient to constitute a defense but significantly reduced the defendant's culpability.
2. The defendant was a passive participant or played a minor role in the commission of the offense.
3. The defendant was suffering from a mental or physical condition that was insufficient to constitute a defense but significantly reduced the defendant's culpability for the offense.
4. The defendant's age, immaturity, or limited mental capacity at the time of commission of the offense significantly reduced the defendant's culpability for the offense.
5. The defendant has made substantial or full restitution to the victim.
6. The victim was more than 16 years of age and was a voluntary participant in the defendant's conduct or consented to it.
7. The defendant aided in the apprehension of another felon or testified truthfully on behalf of the prosecution in another prosecution of a felony.
8. The defendant acted under strong provocation, or the relationship between the defendant and the victim was otherwise extenuating.
9. The defendant could not reasonably foresee that the defendant's conduct would cause or threaten serious bodily harm or fear, or the defendant exercised caution to avoid such consequences.
10. The defendant reasonably believed that the defendant's conduct was legal.
11. Prior to arrest or at an early stage of the criminal process, the defendant voluntarily acknowledged wrongdoing in connection with the offense to a law enforcement officer.
12. The defendant has been a person of good character or has had a good reputation in the community in which the defendant lives.
13. The defendant is a minor and has reliable supervision available.
14. The defendant has been honorably discharged from the United States armed services.
15. The defendant has accepted responsibility for the defendant's criminal conduct.
16. The defendant has entered and is currently involved in or has successfully completed a drug treatment program or an alcohol treatment program subsequent to arrest and prior to trial.
17. The defendant supports the defendant's family.
18. The defendant has a support system in the community.
19. The defendant has a positive employment history or is gainfully employed.
20. The defendant has a good treatment prognosis, and a workable treatment plan is available.
21. Any other mitigating factor reasonably related to the purposes of sentences.

SOURCE: G.S. 15A-1340.16(e).

Table 5
Misdemeanor Sentence Dispositions and Prison/Jail Term Ranges
A = active punishment I = intermediate punishment C = community punishment

Misdemeanor Offense Class (Fine)	Level I No Prior Convictions	Level II 1 to 4 Prior Convictions	Level III 5 or More Prior Convictions
Class A1 (fine discretionary) offense on or after 12/1/95	C/I/A 1–60 days	C/I/A 1–75 days	C/I/A 1–150 days
Class 1 (fine discretionary)	C 1–45 days	C/I/A 1–45 days	C/I/A 1–120 days
Class 2 (maximum fine $1,000)	C 1–30 days	C/I 1–45 days	C/I/A 1–60 days
Class 3 (maximum fine $200)	C 1–10 days	C/I 1–15 days	C/I/A 1–20 days

SOURCE: G.S. 15A-1340.23(c).

Table 6
Felonies (Class F through I) and Misdemeanors
Subject to Restitution Requirements under Crime Victims' Rights Act

Statute	Description of Offense	Punishment
14-16.6(b)	Assault with deadly weapon on executive or legislative officer	Class F felony
14-16.6(c)	Assault inflicting serious bodily injury on executive or legislative officer	Class F felony
14-18	Involuntary manslaughter	Class F felony
14-32.1(e)	Aggravated assault on handicapped person	Class F felony
14-32.2(b)(3)	Patient abuse: conduct resulting in serious bodily injury	Class F felony
14-32.3(a)	Abuse by caretaker of disabled/elder adult in domestic setting:	
	resulting in serious injury	Class F felony
	resulting in injury	Class H felony
14-32.3(b)	Neglect by caretaker of disabled/elder adult in domestic setting:	
	resulting in serious injury	Class G felony
	resulting in injury	Class I felony
14-32.3(c)	Exploitation by caretaker of disabled/elder adult in domestic setting: resulting in loss of more than $1,000	Class H felony
14-32.4	Assault inflicting serious bodily injury	Class F felony
14-33(a)	Simple assault, simple assault and battery, or simple affray	Class 2 misdemeanor*
14-33(c)(1)	Assault:	
	inflicting serious injury	Class A1 misdemeanor*
	with deadly weapon	Class A1 misdemeanor*
14-33(c)(2)	Assault on female	Class A1 misdemeanor*
14-33.2	Habitual misdemeanor assault	Class H felony
14-34	Assault by pointing gun	Class A1 misdemeanor*
14-34.2	Assault with deadly weapon on government official or on company or campus police officer	Class F felony
14-34.6(b)	Assault on firefighter or emergency personnel:	
	inflicting serious bodily injury	Class I felony
	with deadly weapon other than firearm	Class I felony
14-34.6(c)	Assault with firearm on firefighter or emergency personnel	Class F felony
14-41	Abduction of minor	Class F felony

Table continues on next page.

Table 6
[continued]

Statute	Description of Offense	Punishment
14-43.2	Involuntary servitude	Class F felony
14-43.3	Felonious restraint	Class F felony
14-51, -52	Second-degree burglary	Class G felony
14-58	Second-degree arson	Class G felony
14-87.1	Common-law robbery	Class G felony
14-134.3(a)	Domestic criminal trespass	Class 1 misdemeanor*
14-190.17	Second-degree sexual exploitation of minor	Class F felony
14-190.17A	Third-degree sexual exploitation of minor	Class I felony
14-190.19	Participating in prostitution of minor	Class F felony
14-202.1	Taking, or attempting to take, indecent liberties with child	Class F felony
14-277.3	Stalking:	
	First offense	Class 1 misdemeanor*
	While court order in effect prohibiting similar behavior	Class A1 misdemeanor*
	Second or subsequent conviction within 5 years	Class I felony
14-288.9	Assault on emergency personnel: with dangerous weapon or substance	Class F felony
20-138.5	Habitual impaired driving	Class F felony
20-141.4(a1)	Felony death by vehicle	Class G felony

NOTE: The restitution provisions governing sentencing for crimes subject to the Crime Victims' Rights Act (discussed *supra* pp. 9–10) apply to offenses committed on or after Dec. 1, 1998. This table does not show the punishments in effect for offenses committed before that date.

All Class A through E felonies (not listed in this table) are subject to the Crime Victims' Rights Act. An attempt to commit a Class A through E felony or one of the Class F through I felonies listed here is also subject to the Crime Victims' Rights Act if the attempt is punishable as a felony. Unless a different classification is otherwise stated, an attempt to commit a felony is punishable one class lower than the felony attempted. *See* G.S. 14-2.5. An attempt to commit a Class I felony is normally a Class 1 misdemeanor, so it is normally not subject to the Crime Victims' Rights Act.

*A misdemeanor is subject to the Crime Victims' Rights Act only if the defendant and victim have a personal relationship as defined in G.S. 50B-1(b).

SOURCE: G.S. 15A-830(a)(7), -834.

Part 1
Punishment Chart for North Carolina Crimes

Detailed Table of Contents

*The headings in the "Punishment Chart for Crimes" are drawn from the North Carolina General Statutes. The chapter headings refer to chapters in the General Statutes, the bracketed headings refer to subchapters, and the headings below each bracketed heading refer to articles. Chapter and article headings are shown in the body of the punishment chart; the subchapter references do not appear in the punishment chart but are included here to show how the articles in Chapter 14 are organized.

Description of Punishment Chart for Crimes

The "Punishment Chart for North Carolina Crimes" is current through the 1998 session of the General Assembly. It gives the current punishment, as of the close of the 1998 session, for the offenses listed in the chart. It also indicates any punishment changes enacted by the General Assembly for offenses committed on or after October 1, 1994, the date structured sentencing took effect. Thus for the offenses listed in the chart, the punishments are stated for the entire period that structured sentencing has been in effect. For example, voluntary manslaughter is currently a Class D felony and is so shown in the chart. For offenses committed on or after October 1, 1994, and before December 1, 1997, voluntary manslaughter was a Class E felony, and this information is also provided. Not shown, however, is the punishment for voluntary manslaughter (and other offenses) if committed before October 1, 1994, when the Fair Sentencing Act was in effect.

The chart does not include all crimes under North Carolina law, but it is intended to include the crimes that appear most frequently on the criminal dockets of district and superior courts. The chart includes some offenses from Chapter 20 of the General Statutes—those closely related to other offenses listed in the chart. For the most part, however, Chapter 20 violations are listed in the "Punishment Chart for North Carolina Motor Vehicle Offenses," which appears in Part 2 of this book.

The chart is divided into three columns and is organized numerically, by statute number. (A detailed alphabetical index appears at the end of the chart.) The first column lists the statutory reference for the offense. The second column contains a brief description of the offense. The description is intended to provide sufficient information to identify the offense; it does not purport to list all of the elements. The third column indicates the current class of the offense. Where additional information is relevant to the punishment for a particular offense, the information is included in the footnotes. General information about the punishments for different classes of offenses is contained in the Introduction, which describes how sentences are determined under structured sentencing.

Punishment Chart for North Carolina Crimes

Statute	Description of Offense	Punishment
Chapter 5A: Contempt[1]		
5A-11(a), -12(a)	Criminal contempt, generally	Censure, imprisonment up to 30 days, fine up to $500, or combination thereof[2]
5A-11(a)(8), -12(a)	Criminal contempt by willful refusal to testify after being granted immunity	Censure, imprisonment up to 6 months, fine up to $500, or combination thereof
5A-11(a)(9a), -12(a)	Criminal contempt by willful refusal to comply with condition of probation	Censure, imprisonment up to 30 days, fine up to $500, or combination thereof
5A-12(a)	Criminal contempt by failure to comply with nontestimonial identification order	Censure, imprisonment up to 90 days, fine up to $500, or combination thereof

1. Although criminal contempt is characterized as a crime, it is not clear that it constitutes a "misdemeanor." *See generally* Blue Jeans Corp. v. Amalgamated Clothing Workers of Am., 275 N.C. 503, 508, 169 S.E.2d 867, 870 (1969) (characterizing criminal contempt as *sui generis, i.e.*, one of a kind). If considered a misdemeanor, however, a criminal contempt punishable by imprisonment of up to 30 days would constitute a Class 3 misdemeanor, and a criminal contempt punishable by imprisonment of up to 6 months would constitute a Class 2 misdemeanor. *See* G.S. 14-3(a) (designating classes of misdemeanors for which a punishment, but no classification, is stated).

2. G.S. 5A-12(b) provides that a fine or imprisonment may not be imposed unless the behavior was either willfully contemptuous or preceded by a clear warning by the court that the conduct was improper. These limitations do not apply to publication of false reports of court proceedings under G.S. 5A-11(5) or to jury tampering under G.S. 5A-11(9).

G.S. 5A-12(c) authorizes the judge to reduce or withdraw the sentence imposed at any time "if warranted by the conduct of the contemnor and the ends of justice."

G.S. 5A-12(d) states that a person may be held in both criminal and civil contempt for the same conduct, but that the total period of imprisonment for the same conduct is limited as provided in G.S. 5A-21(c). Pursuant to that section, the total period of imprisonment may not exceed the period during which the contemnor may be imprisoned for either civil contempt or criminal contempt under G.S. 5A-12(a), whichever is greater.

Statute	Description of Offense	Punishment

Chapter 14: Criminal Law

Article 1: Felonies and Misdemeanors[3]

Statute	Description of Offense	Punishment
14-2.4(a)	Conspiracy to commit felony	Unless different classification stated, punishable one class lower than felony defendant conspired to commit[4]
14-2.4(b)	Conspiracy to commit misdemeanor	Unless different classification stated, punishable one class lower than misdemeanor defendant conspired to commit[5]
14-2.5	Attempt to commit felony or misdemeanor	Unless different classification stated, punishable one class lower than offense attempted[6]
14-2.6(a)	Solicitation to commit felony	Unless different classification stated, punishable two classes lower than felony solicited[7]
14-2.6(b)	Solicitation to commit misdemeanor	Unless different classification stated, punishable as Class 3 misdemeanor
14-3(a)	Misdemeanors without a specific classification and punishment	Class 1 misdemeanor[8]

3. Subject to certain exceptions, G.S. 14-2.2 provides that if a person uses, displays, or threatens to use or display a firearm during the commission of a Class A through E felony, a term of imprisonment of 60 months must be imposed in addition to the punishment for the underlying felony. Using a firearm in this manner is not a crime; it is instead a circumstance that results in an enhanced punishment upon conviction of the underlying felony. For a discussion of this provision, see "Introduction: Structured Sentencing and Related Laws," *supra* pp. 11–12.

A firearm used in the commission or attempted commission of any felony is subject to forfeiture as provided in G.S. 14-2.2(c). Property acquired as a result of a felony other than a nonwillful homicide is subject to forfeiture as provided in G.S. 14-2.3.

4. Unless a different classification is stated, conspiracy to commit a Class A or B1 felony is a Class B2 felony, conspiracy to commit a Class B2 felony is a Class C felony, and conspiracy to commit a Class I felony is a Class 1 misdemeanor. *See* G.S. 14-2.4(a).

5. Unless a different classification is stated, conspiracy to commit a Class 3 misdemeanor is a Class 3 misdemeanor. *See* G.S. 14-2.4(b).

6. Unless a different classification is stated, attempt to commit a Class A or B1 felony is a Class B2 felony, attempt to commit a Class B2 felony is a Class C felony, attempt to commit a Class I felony is a Class 1 misdemeanor, and attempt to commit a Class 3 misdemeanor is a Class 3 misdemeanor. *See* G.S. 14-2.5.

7. Unless a different classification is stated, solicitation to commit a Class A or B1 felony is a Class C felony, solicitation to commit a Class B2 felony is a Class D felony, solicitation to commit a Class H felony is a Class 1 misdemeanor, and solicitation to commit a Class I felony is a Class 2 misdemeanor. *See* G.S. 14-2.6(a).

8. Misdemeanors with specific punishments but without specific classifications are punishable as follows: (1) as Class 1 misdemeanors if punishable by more than 6 months imprisonment; (2) as Class 2 misdemeanors if punishable by more than 30 days but not more than 6 months imprisonment; and (3) as Class 3 misdemeanors if punishable by imprisonment of 30 days or less or by a fine only. *See* G.S. 14-3(a).

Statute	Description of Offense	Punishment
14-3(b)	Misdemeanors that are infamous, done in secrecy and malice, or committed with deceit and intent to defraud	If no specific punishment prescribed, punishable as Class H felony[9]
14-3(c)	Misdemeanors committed because of the victim's race, color, religion, nationality, or country of origin	Class 2 or 3 misdemeanor committed for proscribed reason punishable as Class 1 misdemeanor; Class A1 or 1 misdemeanor committed for proscribed reason punishable as Class I felony
14-4(a)	Violation of local ordinance, except those in 14-4(b)	Class 3 misdemeanor[10]
14-4(b)	Violation of local ordinance regulating operation or parking of vehicles	Infraction, punishable by penalty up to $50

Article 2: Principals and Accessories

Statute	Description of Offense	Punishment
14-5.2	Accessory to felony before the fact	Punishable as principal[11]
14-7	Accessory to felony after fact	Unless different classification stated, punishable two classes lower than felony committed by principal[12]

9. A misdemeanor may not be elevated to a felony under this statute unless the indictment specifically alleges that the offense was infamous, done in secrecy or malice, or done with deceit and intent to defraud. *See, e.g.,* State v. Bell, 121 N.C. App. 700, 468 S.E.2d 484 (1996).

Before adoption of structured sentencing, the courts considered whether attempt and solicitation crimes could be considered infamous. *See, e.g.*, State v. Glidden, 317 N.C. 557, 346 S.E.2d 470 (1986) (general test for determining whether misdemeanor is "infamous" and punishable as a felony); State v. Huff, 56 N.C. App. 721, 289 S.E.2d 604 (1982) (solicitation to commit perjury is infamous misdemeanor); State v. Tyner, 50 N.C. App. 206, 272 S.E.2d 626 (1980) (solicitation to commit crime against nature is *not* infamous misdemeanor). Under structured sentencing, this inquiry is moot. Attempt and solicitation now have specific punishments (under G.S. 14-2.5 and -2.6), removing them from the class of offenses for which no specific punishment is prescribed and therefore from the operation of G.S. 14-3(b). Conspiracy to commit a misdemeanor likewise cannot be elevated to a felony under G.S. 14-3(b).

10. G.S. 14-4(a) allows a fine of up to $500 for an ordinance violation if the ordinance so provides. If the ordinance does not expressly provide for a fine greater than $50, the fine may not exceed $50.

11. In 1981 the General Assembly abolished the distinction between accessories before the fact and principals in the commission of felonies. Under G.S. 14-5.2 persons who would have been guilty of accessory before the fact under former law are now punished as principals. G.S. 14-5.2 creates one exception to this rule: If a person who would have been convicted of accessory before the fact under former law is convicted of a capital offense, and his or her conviction is based solely on the uncorroborated testimony of one or more principals, co-conspirators, or accessories to the crime, the defendant shall be guilty of a Class B2 felony. Even if this exception is not applicable, it would be unconstitutional in certain circumstances to impose the death penalty on a person who might otherwise be an accessory before the fact to a capital offense. *See* Tison v. Arizona, 481 U.S. 137, 107 S. Ct. 1676, 95 L. Ed. 2d 127 (1987); Enmund v. Florida, 458 U.S. 782, 102 S. Ct. 3368, 73 L. Ed. 2d 1140 (1982); N.C.P.J.I.—Crim. 150.10 (June 1997).

No such distinction is made between principals and accessories before the fact with respect to misdemeanors. Unless otherwise provided, persons who participate in misdemeanors "are indictable and punishable as principals." State v. Bennett, 237 N.C. 749, 752, 76 S.E.2d 42, 43 (1953).

12. Unless a different classification is stated, accessory after the fact to a Class A or B1 felony is a Class C felony, accessory after the fact to a Class B2 felony is a Class D felony, accessory after the fact to a Class H felony is a Class 1

Statute	Description of Offense	Punishment
Article 2A: Habitual Felons		
14-7.1 to -7.6	Habitual felon	Class C felony[13]
Article 2B: Violent Habitual Felons		
14-7.7 to -7.12	Violent habitual felon	Life imprisonment without parole[14]
Article 2C: Continuing Criminal Enterprise		
14-7.20	Continuing criminal enterprise	Class H felony[15]
Article 6: Homicide		
14-17	Murder:	
	First-degree	Class A felony[16]
	Second-degree	Class B2 felony

misdemeanor, and accessory after the fact to a Class I felony is a Class 2 misdemeanor. *See* G.S. 14-7. For offenses committed on or after Oct. 1, 1994, and before Dec. 1, 1997, accessory after the fact to a felony was a Class H felony.

A participant in a crime cannot be an accessory after the fact to that crime. See State v. McIntosh, 260 N.C. 749, 133 S.E.2d 652 (1963). In the absence of a statute providing otherwise, a person apparently may not be convicted of being an accessory after the fact to a misdemeanor. *See* 2 Wayne R. LaFave & Austin W. Scott, Jr., Substantive Criminal Law § 6.9(a), at 167 (1986); Rollin M. Perkins & Ronald N. Boyce, Criminal Law 726 (3d ed. 1982).

13. Being a habitual felon is not a crime. It is a status that subjects the defendant to an enhanced punishment upon conviction of a felony. *See* State v. Allen, 292 N.C. 431, 233 S.E.2d 585 (1977). G.S. 14-7.6 provides that, upon conviction as a habitual felon, the defendant is sentenced as a Class C felon for the underlying felony (except if the conviction is for a Class A, B1, or B2 felony). G.S. 14-7.6 also provides that the sentence must run consecutively with and must begin to run at the expiration of any sentence being served by the person at the time of sentencing. When two or more offenses are being disposed of in the same proceeding, however, the court apparently is not required to impose consecutive sentences. *See* State v. Thomas, 85 N.C. App. 319, 354 S.E.2d 891 (1987) (construing similar consecutive sentencing provisions); State v. Crain, 73 N.C. App. 269, 326 S.E.2d 120 (1985) (to same effect). For a discussion of calculating the prior record level of a person found to be a habitual felon, see "Introduction: Structured Sentencing and Related Laws," *supra* pp. 10–11.

14. Being a violent habitual felon is not a crime. It is a status that subjects the defendant to an enhanced punishment upon conviction of a third "violent felony" as defined in G.S. 14-7.7. Upon conviction as a violent habitual felon, the defendant must be sentenced to life without parole, except where the death penalty is imposed. G.S. 14-7.12 provides that the enhanced sentence may not be suspended; the person may not be placed on probation for the sentence; and the sentence must run consecutively with and must begin to run at the expiration of any sentence being served by the person at the time of sentencing. For a further discussion of these provisions, see "Introduction: Structured Sentencing and Related Laws," *supra* p. 11.

15. G.S. 14-7.20(b) provides that a person convicted of engaging in a continuing criminal enterprise forfeits to the state his or her profits from and interest in the enterprise. G.S. 14-7.20 applies to offenses committed on or after Dec. 1, 1995.

16. A person under 17 years of age at the time of the offense is not eligible for the death penalty unless the offense is committed while the person is serving a prison sentence for a prior murder or while the person is on escape from such a sentence. *See* G.S. 14-17. For a discussion of pardon eligibility for a person sentenced to life without parole, see "Introduction: Structured Sentencing and Related Laws," *supra* p. 10.

Statute	Description of Offense	Punishment
14-18	Manslaughter:	
	Voluntary	Class D felony[17]
	Involuntary	Class F felony
14-18.2(b)	Injuring pregnant woman during commission of felony	Punishable one class higher than felony committed[18]
14-18.2(c)	Injuring pregnant woman during commission of misdemeanor that is act of domestic violence	Punishable one class higher than misdemeanor committed[19]

Article 7A: Rape and Other Sex Offenses

Statute	Description of Offense	Punishment
14-27.2	First-degree rape	Class B1 felony[20]
14-27.3	Second-degree rape	Class C felony
14-27.4	First-degree sexual offense	Class B1 felony[21]
14-27.5	Second-degree sexual offense	Class C felony
14-27.7	Sexual act:	
	by parental substitute with minor	Class E felony
	by custodian with victim of any age	Class E felony
14-27.7A	Statutory rape or statutory sexual offense with person 13, 14, or 15 years old:[22]	
	when defendant is at least 6 years older than person	Class B1 felony
	when defendant is more than 4 but less than 6 years older than person	Class C felony

Article 8: Assaults

Statute	Description of Offense	Punishment
14-28	Malicious castration	Class C felony
14-29	Castration or maiming	Class E felony
14-30	Malicious maiming	Class C felony

17. For offenses committed on or after Oct. 1, 1994, and before Dec. 1, 1997, this offense was a Class E felony.

18. G.S. 14-18.2 applies to offenses committed on or after Jan. 1, 1999.

19. A defendant who commits this offense during the commission of a Class A1 misdemeanor is guilty of a Class I felony. G.S. 14-18.2 applies to offenses committed on or after Jan. 1, 1999.

20. Effective for offenses committed on or after Jan. 1, 1999, G.S. 15A-1340.16B provides for life imprisonment without parole for a Class B1 felony if it was committed against a person 13 or younger, the defendant has at least one prior conviction for a Class B1 felony, and there are no mitigating factors. If one or more of these conditions is not met, the court must sentence the defendant according to the regular structured sentencing rules. For a further discussion of this provision, see "Introduction: Structured Sentencing and Related Laws," *supra* p. 10.

21. *See* note 20.

22. G.S. 14-27.7A applies to offenses committed on or after Dec. 1, 1995. For the punishment for a Class B1 felony, *see* note 20.

Statute	Description of Offense	Punishment
14-30.1	Malicious acid throwing	Class E felony
14-31	Malicious assault and battery in secret manner with deadly weapon and intent to kill	Class E felony
14-32(a)	Assault with deadly weapon with intent to kill, inflicting serious injury	Class C felony
14-32(b)	Assault with deadly weapon, inflicting serious injury	Class E felony
14-32(c)	Assault with deadly weapon with intent to kill	Class E felony
14-32.1(e)	Aggravated assault on handicapped person	Class F felony
14-32.1(f)	Simple assault on handicapped person	Class 1 misdemeanor
14-32.2(b)(1)	Patient abuse: intentional conduct resulting in death	Class C felony
14-32.2(b)(2)	Patient abuse: culpably negligent conduct resulting in death	Class E felony
14-32.2(b)(3)	Patient abuse: conduct resulting in serious bodily injury	Class F felony
14-32.3(a)	Abuse by caretaker of disabled or elder adult residing in domestic setting:[23]	
	resulting in serious injury	Class F felony
	resulting in injury	Class H felony
14-32.3(b)	Neglect by caretaker of disabled or elder adult residing in domestic setting:[24]	
	resulting in serious injury	Class G felony
	resulting in injury	Class I felony
14-32.3(c)	Exploitation by caretaker of disabled or elder adult residing in domestic setting:[25]	
	resulting in loss of money or property of more than $1,000	Class H felony
	resulting in loss of money or property up to $1,000	Class 1 misdemeanor
14-32.4	Assault inflicting serious bodily injury	Class F felony[26]
14-33(a)	Simple assault, simple assault and battery, or simple affray	Class 2 misdemeanor[27]
14-33(b)(9)	Assault and battery on sports official	Class 1 misdemeanor

23. G.S. 14-32.3 applies to offenses committed on or after Dec. 1, 1995.

24. *See* note 23.

25. *See* note 23.

26. G.S. 14-32.4 applies to offenses committed on or after Jan. 1, 1997.

27. For offenses committed on or after Oct. 1, 1994, and before Dec. 1, 1995, this offense was a Class 1 misdemeanor.

Statute	Description of Offense	Punishment
14-33(c)(1)	Assault:[28]	
	inflicting serious injury	Class A1 misdemeanor
	with deadly weapon	Class A1 misdemeanor
14-33(c)(2)	Assault on female	Class A1 misdemeanor[29]
14-33(c)(3)	Assault on child under 12	Class A1 misdemeanor[30]
14-33(c)(4)	Assault on government official	Class A1 misdemeanor[31]
14-33(c)(5)	Assault on school bus personnel	Class A1 misdemeanor[32]
14-33.2	Habitual misdemeanor assault	Class H felony[33]
14-34	Assault by pointing gun	Class A1 misdemeanor[34]
14-34.1	Discharging or attempting to discharge firearm into occupied property	Class E felony
14-34.2	Assault with deadly weapon on government official or on company or campus police officer	Class F felony
14-34.4(a)	Tampering with food, drugs, or cosmetics with intent to cause serious injury	Class C felony
14-34.4(b)	Threatening to tamper with food, drugs, or cosmetics with intent to extort	Class C felony
14-34.5(a)	Assault with firearm on law-enforcement, probation, or parole officer	Class E felony[35]
14-34.5(b)	Assault with firearm on detention facility employee	Class E felony[36]
14-34.6(a)	Assault on firefighter or emergency personnel	Class A1 misdemeanor[37]

28. For offenses committed on or after Oct. 1, 1994, and before Dec. 1, 1995, this offense was a Class 1 misdemeanor, punishable under former G.S. 14-33(b).

29. *See* note 28.

30. *See* note 28.

31. *See* note 28.

32. G.S. 14-33(c)(5) applies to offenses committed on or after Dec. 1, 1995.

33. G.S. 14-33.2 applies to offenses committed on or after Dec. 1, 1995.

34. For offenses committed on or after Oct. 1, 1994, and before Dec. 1, 1995, this offense was a Class 1 misdemeanor.

35. G.S. 14-34.5(a) applies to offenses committed against law-enforcement officers on or after Dec. 1, 1995, and to offenses committed against probation or parole officers on or after Dec. 1, 1997. Assault with a firearm on such officers on or after Oct. 1, 1994, and before the applicable effective date was a Class F felony, punishable under G.S. 14-34.2.

36. G.S. 14-34.5(b) applies to offenses committed on or after Dec. 1, 1997. Assault with a firearm on such an official on or after Oct. 1, 1994, and before Dec. 1, 1997, was a Class F felony, punishable under G.S. 14-34.2.

37. G.S. 14-34.6 applies to offenses committed against emergency personnel on or after Dec. 1, 1995, and to offenses committed against firefighters on or after Mar. 26, 1997.

Statute	Description of Offense	Punishment
14-34.6(b)	Assault on firefighter or emergency personnel:[38]	
	inflicting serious bodily injury	Class I felony
	with deadly weapon other than firearm	Class I felony
14-34.6(c)	Assault with firearm on firefighter or emergency personnel	Class F felony[39]
14-34.7(a)	Assault inflicting serious bodily injury on law-enforcement, probation, or parole officer	Class F felony[40]
14-34.7(b)	Assault inflicting serious bodily injury on detention facility employee	Class F felony[41]

Article 9: Hazing

Statute	Description of Offense	Punishment
14-35	Hazing	Class 2 misdemeanor
14-36	Failure to expel student convicted of hazing	Class 1 misdemeanor

Article 10: Kidnapping and Abduction[42]

Statute	Description of Offense	Punishment
14-39	Kidnapping:[43]	
	First-degree	Class C felony
	Second-degree	Class E felony
14-41	Abduction of minor	Class F felony[44]
14-43.2	Involuntary servitude	Class F felony
14-43.3	Felonious restraint	Class F felony

Article 11: Abortion and Kindred Offenses

Statute	Description of Offense	Punishment
14-44	Using drugs or instruments with intent to cause abortion	Class H felony[45]

38. *See* note 37.

39. *See* note 37.

40. G.S. 14-34.7(a) applies to offenses committed against law-enforcement officers on or after Dec. 1, 1996, and to offenses committed against probation or parole officers on or after Dec. 1, 1997.

41. G.S. 14-34.7(b) applies to offenses committed on or after Dec. 1, 1997.

42. The common law also makes false imprisonment a misdemeanor. It would be punishable as a Class 1 misdemeanor under G.S. 14-3(a) (misdemeanors without specific classification and punishment).

43. G.S. 14-39(c) provides that any firm or corporation convicted of kidnapping shall be fined from $5,000 to $100,000, and its charter and right to do business in North Carolina shall be forfeited.

44. The definition of this offense was rewritten for offenses committed on or after Jan. 1, 1997. Before this change, the person abducted must have been under 14 and residing with certain relatives, with a guardian, or at a school.

45. G.S. 14-45.1 provides that, notwithstanding G.S. 14-44 and -45, it is not unlawful for abortions to be performed under certain conditions.

Statute	Description of Offense	Punishment
14-45	Using drugs or instruments with intent to produce miscarriage or injure pregnant woman	Class I felony[46]
14-46	Concealing birth of child:	
	Concealing	Class I felony
	Aiding or abetting another in concealing	Class 1 misdemeanor

Article 12: Libel and Slander

Statute	Description of Offense	Punishment
14-47	Communicating libelous matter to newspaper	Class 2 misdemeanor

Article 13: Malicious Injury or Damage by Use of Explosive or Incendiary Device or Material

Statute	Description of Offense	Punishment
14-49(a)	Malicious use of explosive or incendiary device to injure another	Class D felony
14-49(b)	Malicious use of explosive or incendiary device to damage property	Class G felony
14-49(b1)	Malicious use of explosive or incendiary device to damage building of worship	Class E felony[47]
14-49.1	Malicious use of explosive or incendiary device to damage occupied property	Class D felony

Article 14: Burglary and Other Housebreakings

Statute	Description of Offense	Punishment
14-51, -52	Burglary:	
	First-degree	Class D felony
	Second-degree	Class G felony
14-53	Breaking out of dwelling house	Class D felony
14-54(a)	Breaking or entering building with intent to commit felony or larceny	Class H felony
14-54(b)	Misdemeanor breaking or entering building	Class 1 misdemeanor
14-55	Preparation to commit burglary	Class I felony[48]
14-56	Breaking or entering car, boat, airplane, etc., with intent to commit felony or larceny	Class I felony[49]

46. *See* note 45.

47. G.S. 14-49(b1) applies to offenses committed on or after June 21, 1996. Bombing of a religious structure on or after Oct. 1, 1994, and before June 21, 1996, was a Class G felony, punishable under G.S. 14-49(b).

48. G.S. 14-55 creates three separate offenses: (1) possession of burglar's tools without lawful excuse; (2) being in a building with intent to commit any felony or larceny; and (3) being armed with intent to break or enter a building and to commit a felony or larceny therein. *See* State v. Garrett, 263 N.C. 773, 140 S.E.2d 315 (1965).

49. This offense includes breaking out after committing a felony or larceny. *See* G.S. 14-56.

Statute	Description of Offense	Punishment
14-56.1	Breaking into coin/currency-operated machine:	
	First offense	Class 1 misdemeanor
	Subsequent offense	Class I felony
14-56.2	Damaging coin/currency-operated machine	Class 1 misdemeanor
14-56.3	Breaking into paper currency machine:	
	First offense	Class 1 misdemeanor
	Subsequent offense	Class I felony
14-57	Burglary with explosive	Class D felony

Article 15: Arson and Other Burnings

Statute	Description of Offense	Punishment
14-58	Arson:	
	First-degree	Class D felony[50]
	Second-degree	Class G felony
14-59	Burning public building	Class F felony
14-60	Burning educational institution	Class F felony
14-61	Burning bridges, certain buildings	Class F felony
14-62	Burning uninhabited dwellings, certain other buildings	Class F felony
14-62.1	Burning building in process of construction	Class H felony
14-62.2	Burning church, chapel, or meetinghouse	Class E felony[51]
14-63	Burning boat or barge	Class H felony
14-64	Burning ginhouse or tobacco house	Class H felony
14-65	Burning dwelling house owned or occupied by defendant	Class H felony
14-66	Burning personal property	Class H felony
14-67.1	Burning building not otherwise covered by statute	Class H felony
14-69.1	Making false report of destructive device in any structure or vehicle	Class H felony[52]
14-69.2	Perpetrating hoax by use of false bomb	Class H felony[53]

50. This offense includes the crime set out in G.S. 14-58.2, which provides that a person is guilty of first-degree arson if he or she "willfully and maliciously burn[s] any mobile home . . . which is the dwelling house of another and which is occupied at the time of the burning. . . ."

51. G.S. 14-62.2 applies to offenses committed on or after June 21, 1996. Burning of a religious structure on or after Oct. 1, 1994, and before June 21, 1996, was a Class F felony, punishable under G.S. 14-62.

52. For offenses committed on or after Oct. 1, 1994, and before Dec. 1, 1997, making a false report of a destructive device in a structure other than a hospital was a Class 1 misdemeanor, while making a false report of a destructive device in a hospital was a Class 1 misdemeanor for a first offense and a Class I felony for a subsequent offense.

53. For offenses committed on or after Oct. 1, 1994, and before Dec. 1, 1997, perpetrating a hoax by use of a false bomb in a structure other than a hospital was a Class 1 misdemeanor, while perpetrating such a hoax in a hospital was a Class 1 misdemeanor for a first offense and a Class I felony for a subsequent offense.

Article 16: Larceny[54]

Statute	Description of Offense	Punishment
14-70, -72(a)	Larceny:	
	of goods valued up to $1,000	Class 1 misdemeanor
	of goods valued over $1,000	Class H felony
14-70, -72(a), -72(b)(1)	Larceny from person	Class H felony
14-70, -72(a), -72(b)(2)	Larceny pursuant to burglary or breaking or entering in violation of 14-51, -53, -54, or -57	Class H felony
14-70, -72(a), -72(b)(3)	Larceny of explosive or incendiary device or substance	Class H felony
14-70, -72(a), -72(b)(4)	Larceny of firearm	Class H felony
14-70, -72(a), -72(b)(5)	Larceny of record or paper in custody of State Archives	Class H felony
14-71, -72(a)	Receiving:	
	stolen goods valued up to $1,000	Class 1 misdemeanor
	stolen goods valued over $1,000	Class H felony
14-71, -72(c)	Receiving:	
	goods stolen from a person	Class H felony
	goods stolen pursuant to burglary or breaking or entering in violation of 14-51, -53, -54, or -57	Class H felony
	stolen explosive or incendiary device or substance	Class H felony
	stolen firearm	Class H felony
	stolen record or paper in custody of State Archives	Class H felony
14-71.1, -72(a)	Possession:	
	of stolen goods valued up to $1,000	Class 1 misdemeanor
	of stolen goods valued over $1,000	Class H felony
14-71.1, -72(c)	Possession:	
	of goods stolen from a person	Class H felony
	of goods stolen pursuant to burglary or breaking or entering in violation of 14-51, -53, -54, or -57	Class H felony
	of stolen explosive or incendiary device or substance	Class H felony
	of stolen firearm	Class H felony
	of stolen record or paper in custody of State Archives	Class H felony

54. Conveyances used to conceal, convey, or transport property in violation of G.S. 14-71 (receiving stolen goods) or -71.1 (possession of stolen goods) or used in the commission of any larceny when the value of the property taken is more than $2,000 are subject to forfeiture as provided in G.S. 14-86.1.

Statute	Description of Offense	Punishment
14-72.1(a), -72.1(e)	Willful concealment of merchandise:	
	First offense	Class 3 misdemeanor[55]
	Second offense within 3 years of conviction of first offense	Class 2 misdemeanor[56]
	Third or subsequent offense within 5 years of two prior convictions	Class 1 misdemeanor[57]
	Subsequent offense not falling into above two categories	Class 3 misdemeanor[58]
14-72.1(d), -72.1(e)	Switching price tags:	
	First offense	Class 3 misdemeanor[59]
	Second offense within 3 years of conviction of first offense	Class 2 misdemeanor[60]
	Third or subsequent offense within 5 years of two prior convictions	Class 1 misdemeanor[61]
	Subsequent offense not falling into above two categories	Class 3 misdemeanor[62]
14-72.1(d1)	Willful concealment of merchandise by lead/aluminum-lined device	Class H felony[63]
14-72.2	Unauthorized use:	
	of motor vehicle, motorboat, or other motor-propelled conveyance	Class 1 misdemeanor
	of aircraft	Class H felony

55. G.S. 14-72.1(e) provides that the term of imprisonment may be suspended only on condition that the defendant perform community service for a term of at least 24 hours. If the judge finds that the defendant is unable to perform community service because of a mental or physical infirmity, the judge may impose such other sentence as he or she finds appropriate, provided the judge sets out the reasons for this finding in the judgment. G.S. 14-72.1(g) contains additional limitations on terms of active imprisonment, but it is unclear how to apply those limitations in light of structured sentencing.

56. G.S. 14-72.1(e) provides that the term of imprisonment may be suspended only on condition that the defendant be imprisoned for at least 72 hours as a condition of special probation, perform community service for at least 72 hours, or both. If the judge finds that the defendant is unable to perform community service because of a mental or physical infirmity, the judge may impose such other sentence as he or she finds appropriate, provided that the judge sets out the reasons for this finding in the judgment. G.S. 14-72.1(g) contains additional limitations on terms of active imprisonment, but it is unclear how to apply those limitations in light of structured sentencing.

57. G.S. 14-72.1(e) provides that the term of imprisonment may be suspended only if a condition of special probation is that the defendant serve a term of imprisonment of at least 11 days. G.S. 14-72.1(g) contains additional limitations on terms of active imprisonment, but it is unclear how to apply those limitations in light of structured sentencing.

58. *See* note 55.

59. *See* note 55.

60. *See* note 56.

61. *See* note 57.

62. *See* note 55.

63. G.S. 14-72.1(d1) applies to offenses committed on or after Dec. 1, 1997.

Statute	Description of Offense	Punishment
14-72.3	Unauthorized removal of shopping cart from shopping premises	Class 3 misdemeanor
14-72.4	Unauthorized taking or sale of labeled milk crate	Class 2 misdemeanor
14-74	Larceny or embezzlement by employee:[64]	
	of less than $100,000	Class H felony
	of $100,000 or more	Class C felony[65]
14-75	Larceny of chose in action	Class H felony
14-75.1	Larceny of secret technical process	Class H felony
14-76	Larceny of public records or papers	Class 1 misdemeanor
14-77	Larceny of will	Class 1 misdemeanor
14-79.1	Larceny of pine straw	Class H felony[66]
14-81(a)	Larceny of horse, mule, swine, or cattle	Class H felony[67]
14-81(a1)	Larceny of a dog	Class I felony[68]
14-82	Temporarily taking horse, mule, or dog	Class 2 misdemeanor

Article 17: Robbery[69]

Statute	Description of Offense	Punishment
14-87	Armed robbery or attempted armed robbery	Class D felony
14-87.1	Common-law robbery	Class G felony
14-88	Train robbery	Class D felony
14-89.1	Safecracking or attempted safecracking	Class I felony

Article 18: Embezzlement

Statute	Description of Offense	Punishment
14-90	Embezzlement by agent or fiduciary:	
	of less than $100,000	Class H felony
	of $100,000 or more	Class C felony[70]

64. G.S. 14-74 does not apply to employees under 16.

65. For offenses committed on or after Oct. 1, 1994, and before Dec. 1, 1997, this offense was a Class H felony.

66. G.S. 14-79.1 applies to offenses committed on or after Dec. 1, 1997.

67. G.S. 14-81(b) provides that the minimum sentence for this offense is probation subject to the following conditions: (1) restitution for the damage or loss caused by the larceny and (2) a fine of not less than the amount of damages or loss caused by the larceny.

68. *See* note 67.

69. Conveyances used in the commission of armed or common-law robbery are subject to forfeiture as provided in G.S. 14-86.1.

70. For offenses committed on or after Oct. 1, 1994, and before Dec. 1, 1997, this offense was a Class H felony.

Statute	Description of Offense	Punishment
14-91	Embezzlement of state property by public officer or employee:	
	of less than $100,000	Class F felony
	of $100,000 or more	Class C felony[71]
14-92	Embezzlement by public officer or trustee:	
	of less than $100,000	Class F felony
	of $100,000 or more	Class C felony[72]
14-93	Embezzlement by treasurer of charitable or religious organization:[73]	
	of less than $100,000	Class H felony
	of $100,000 or more	Class C felony[74]
14-94	Embezzlement by officer of railroad company:	
	of less than $100,000	Class H felony
	of $100,000 or more	Class C felony[75]
14-97	Appropriation of partnership funds by partner:	
	of less than $100,000	Class H felony
	of $100,000 or more	Class C felony[76]
14-98	Embezzlement by surviving partner, with refusal to account for funds:	
	of less than $100,000	Class H felony
	of $100,000 or more	Class C felony[77]
14-99	Embezzlement of taxes by public officer:	
	of less than $100,000	Class F felony
	of $100,000 or more	Class C felony[78]

71. For offenses committed on or after Oct. 1, 1994, and before Dec. 1, 1997, this offense was a Class F felony.

72. *See* note 71.

73. This section creates two offenses applicable to financial officers of benevolent or religious institutions: (1) lending money without consent of the institution and (2) failing to account for money. *See* State v. Dunn, 138 N.C. 672, 50 S.E. 772 (1905).

74. *See* note 70.

75. *See* note 70.

76. *See* note 70.

77. *See* note 70.

78. *See* note 71.

Statute	Description of Offense	Punishment

Article 19: False Pretenses and Cheats

Statute	Description of Offense	Punishment
14-100	Obtaining or attempting to obtain property by false pretenses:	
	of less than $100,000	Class H felony
	of $100,000 or more	Class C felony[79]
14-101	Obtaining signature by false pretenses	Class H felony
14-104	Obtaining advance by false promise to work	Class 2 misdemeanor
14-105	Obtaining advance by false written promise to pay out of designated property	Class 2 misdemeanor
14-106	Obtaining property by worthless check	Class 2 misdemeanor
14-107	Knowingly writing worthless check over $2,000	Class I felony[80]
14-107(1)	Knowingly writing worthless check for $100 or less	Class 2 misdemeanor[81]
14-107(2)	Knowingly writing worthless check over $100 and not more than $2,000	Class 2 misdemeanor[82]
14-107(3)	Knowingly writing worthless check on nonexistent account	Class 1 misdemeanor[83]
14-107(4)	Knowingly writing worthless check on closed account	Class 1 misdemeanor[84]
14-110	Defrauding innkeeper or restaurant owner	Class 2 misdemeanor
14-112	Obtaining merchandise on approval with intent to defraud	Class 2 misdemeanor
14-113	Obtaining money by false representation of physical defect	Class 2 misdemeanor

79. For offenses committed on or after Oct. 1, 1994, and before Dec. 1, 1997, this offense was a Class H felony.

80. G.S. 14-107 provides that the judge, in imposing any sentence other than an active term of imprisonment, may require the defendant to pay as part of the costs a witness fee for each prosecuting witness and to make restitution to the victim for (i) the amount of the check, (ii) any service charges imposed on the payee by a bank for processing the dishonored check, and (iii) any processing fees imposed by the payee in compliance with G.S. 25-3-506.

81. A defendant who has previously been convicted three times of violating G.S. 14-107 shall be punished for this offense as for a Class 1 misdemeanor; if placed on probation, the defendant shall be ordered to refrain from maintaining a checking account or making or uttering a check for 3 years. *See* G.S. 14-107(1). In imposing any sentence other than an active term of imprisonment, the judge may require the defendant to pay costs and make restitution as described in note 80.

82. A defendant who has previously been convicted three times of violating G.S. 14-107 *may* be punished for this offense as for a Class 1 misdemeanor; if placed on probation, the defendant shall be ordered to refrain from maintaining a checking account or making or uttering a check for 3 years. *See* G.S. 14-107(2). In imposing any sentence other than an active term of imprisonment, the judge may require the defendant to pay costs and make restitution as described in note 80.

83. *See* note 80.

84. *See* note 80.

Article 19A: Obtaining Property or Services by False or Fraudulent Use of Credit Device or Other Means[85]

Statute	Description of Offense	Punishment
14-113.1, -113.6	Obtaining or attempting to obtain goods through false telephone number, false credit number, or credit device	Class 2 misdemeanor
14-113.4, -113.6	Avoiding or attempting to avoid lawful charges for telecommunications services	Class 2 misdemeanor
14-113.5, -113.6	Unlawful use of telecommunications services	Class 2 misdemeanor[86]

Article 19B: Financial Transaction Card Crime Act[87]

Statute	Description of Offense	Punishment
14-113.9, -113.17(b)	Theft of financial transaction card	Class I felony
14-113.11, -113.17(b)	Forgery of financial transaction card	Class I felony
14-113.13(a), -113.13(b) -113.17	Financial transaction card fraud:	
	when value obtained in 6-month period is $500 or less	Class 2 misdemeanor
	when value obtained in 6-month period exceeds $500	Class I felony
14-113.13(c), -113.17(a)	False statement on application for financial transaction card	Class 2 misdemeanor
14-113.13(c1), -113.17(a)	False record of sale submitted by person authorized to accept financial transaction card	Class 2 misdemeanor
14-113.13(d), -113.17(a)	False report of loss of financial transaction card	Class 2 misdemeanor
14-113.14, -113.17(b)	Criminal possession of financial transaction card forgery device	Class I felony
14-113.15, -113.17	Criminal receipt of goods or services obtained by financial transaction card fraud:	
	when value obtained in 6-month period is $500 or less	Class 2 misdemeanor
	when value obtained in 6-month period exceeds $500	Class I felony

85. This article does not apply to credit cards. *See* G.S. 14-113.7A.

86. Effective for offenses committed on or after Dec. 1, 1995, G.S. 14-113.5 and -113.6 were revised as follows: G.S. 14-113.5 contains a broader definition of unlawful use of telecommunications services; G.S. 14-113.6(a) provides that a violation of G.S. 14-113.5 is a Class G felony if it involves five or more unlawful telecommunications devices; G.S. 14-113.6(b) provides that a court may order restitution for a violation of G.S. 14-113.5; and G.S. 14-113.6(c) provides that a person or entity aggrieved by a violation may bring a civil action for declaratory relief, compensatory and punitive damages, reasonable investigation expenses, costs of suit, and attorneys' fees as allowed by law.

87. G.S. 14-113.8(4) sets out the statutory definition of financial transaction card. The definition includes credit cards as well as cards used to operate automatic banking devices.

Statute	Description of Offense	Punishment
14-113.15A, -113.17(b)	Criminal factoring of financial transaction card records	Class I felony

Article 20: Frauds

Statute	Description of Offense	Punishment
14-114	Fraudulent disposal or purchase of collateral	Class 2 misdemeanor
14-115	Secreting property to hinder enforcement of security interest	Class 2 misdemeanor
14-118	Blackmail	Class 1 misdemeanor
14-118.1	Simulation of court process in connection with collection of claim, demand, or account	Class 2 misdemeanor
14-118.2	Assisting in obtaining academic credit by fraudulent means	Class 2 misdemeanor
14-118.4	Extortion	Class F felony
14-118.5(a)	Unauthorized interception of cable television service	Class 3 misdemeanor[88]
14-118.5(b)	Unauthorized sale of decoder for cable television signal	Class 3 misdemeanor[89]

Article 21: Forgery[90]

Statute	Description of Offense	Punishment
14-119	Forgery of bank notes, checks, and securities	Class I felony
14-120	Forged instruments:	
	Uttering forged instruments	Class I felony
	Forging endorsement	Class I felony
	Uttering instrument with forged endorsement	Class I felony
14-121	Selling forged securities	Class H felony
14-122	Forgery of deeds, wills, etc.	Class H felony
14-122.1	Falsifying documents issued by school or government agency	Class 1 misdemeanor
14-124	Corporate stock certificates:	
	Forgery	Class I felony
	Uttering	Class I felony

88. G.S. 14-118.5 authorizes a fine up to $500.

89. *See* note 88.

90. Forgery is also a common-law misdemeanor. It would be punishable as a Class 1 misdemeanor under G.S. 14-3(a) (misdemeanors without a specific classification and punishment) unless considered an "infamous" misdemeanor under G.S. 14-3(b), in which case it would be punishable as a Class H felony. *See* State v. Glidden, 317 N.C. 557, 346 S.E.2d 470 (1986) (discusses test for determining whether offense is infamous, done in secrecy and malice, or committed with deceit and intent to defraud).

Statute	Description of Offense	Punishment

Article 22: Damages and Other Offenses against Land and Fixtures

Statute	Description of Offense	Punishment
14-127	Injury to real property	Class 1 misdemeanor
14-128	Injury to trees, crops, lands of another	Class 1 misdemeanor
14-130	Trespass on public lands	Class 1 misdemeanor
14-132(a)(1), -132(d)	Disorderly conduct in or near public building or facility	Class 2 misdemeanor
14-132(a)(2), -132(d)	Defacing or injuring public building or facility	Class 2 misdemeanor
14-132.2(a)	Injuring public school bus	Class 1 misdemeanor
14-132.2(b)	Entering public school bus after being forbidden	Class 2 misdemeanor
14-132.2(c)	Refusing to leave public school bus after demand	Class 2 misdemeanor
14-134.3(a)	Domestic criminal trespass	Class 1 misdemeanor
14-134.3(b)	Domestic criminal trespass on safe house by person with deadly weapon	Class G felony[91]
14-136	Setting fire to grass, brushlands, or woodlands:	
	First offense	Class 2 misdemeanor
	Subsequent offense	Class 1 misdemeanor
	With intent to damage property of another	Class I felony
14-137	Setting fire to woods or fields	Class 2 misdemeanor
14-138.1	Starting fire on grassland, brushland, or woodland and failing to extinguish fire	Class 3 misdemeanor[92]
14-140.1	Burning brush, grass, or other material without watchman	Class 3 misdemeanor[93]
14-144	Injuring house, church, fence, or wall	Class 2 misdemeanor
14-145	Unlawful posting of advertisement	Class 3 misdemeanor
14-148(a)(1), -148(c)	Throwing trash in cemetery	Class 1 misdemeanor[94]
14-148(a)(2), -148(c)	Vandalizing cemetery enclosure, causing less than $1,000 damage	Class 1 misdemeanor[95]
14-148(a)(3), -148(c)	Vandalizing grave marker or ornament, causing less than $1,000 damage	Class 1 misdemeanor[96]

91. G.S. 14-134.3(b) applies to offenses committed on or after Jan. 1, 1999.

92. The punishment for this offense may include a fine from $10 to $50. G.S. 14-138.1 applies to offenses committed on or after June 8, 1995; it replaces G.S. 14-138, which was repealed Oct. 1, 1994.

93. The punishment for this offense may include a fine from $10 to $50. G.S. 14-140.1 applies to offenses committed on or after June 8, 1995; it replaces G.S. 14-140, which was repealed Oct. 1, 1994.

94. G.S. 14-148(c) provides that the court shall consider, as an alternative to imposition of a fine or jail term, the appropriateness of restitution or reparation as a condition of probation.

95. *See* note 94.

96. *See* note 94.

Statute	Description of Offense	Punishment
14-149(a)(1)	Desecrating grave	Class I felony
14-149(a)(2)	Vandalizing cemetery enclosure, causing more than $1,000 damage	Class I felony
14-149(a)(3)	Vandalizing grave marker or ornament, causing more than $1,000 damage	Class I felony
14-151.1	Interfering with electric, gas, or water meter	Class 1 misdemeanor
14-158	Interfering with telephone lines	Class 2 misdemeanor
14-159.1	Contaminating public water system	Class C felony
14-159.2(a)(1), -159.2(b)	Unauthorized entry into animal research facility with intent to disrupt operations, damage facility, release animal, or interfere with care of animals	Class 1 misdemeanor[97]
14-159.2(a)(2), -159.2(b)	Damaging animal research facility	Class 1 misdemeanor[98]
14-159.2(a)(3), -159.2(b)	Unauthorized release of animal from animal research facility	Class 1 misdemeanor[99]
14-159.2(a)(4), -159.2(b)	Interfering with care of animal in animal research facility	Class 1 misdemeanor[100]
14-159.3	Trespassing with motorized all-terrain vehicle	Class 2 misdemeanor[101]

Article 22A: Trespassing Upon "Posted" Property to Hunt, Fish, Trap, or Remove Pine Needles/Straw

Statute	Description of Offense	Punishment
14-159.6(a)	Hunting or fishing on posted property	Class 2 misdemeanor
14-159.6(b)	Raking or removing pine straw on posted property	Class 1 misdemeanor[102]

Article 22B: First and Second Degree Trespass[103]

Statute	Description of Offense	Punishment
14-159.12	First-degree trespass	Class 2 misdemeanor
14-159.13	Second-degree trespass	Class 3 misdemeanor

97. G.S. 14-159.2(c) provides that a violation of G.S. 14-159.2(a) involving release of an animal with an infectious disease is a Class I felony. G.S. 14-159.2(d) provides that, as a condition of probation, the court may order a person convicted under G.S. 14-159.2 to make restitution for damages resulting from the violation, including such costs as replacing animals and equipment.

98. *See* note 97.

99. *See* note 97.

100. *See* note 97.

101. G.S. 14-159.3 applies to offenses committed on or after Dec. 1, 1997.

102. G.S. 14-159.6(b) applies to offenses committed on or after Dec. 1, 1997.

103. Forcible trespass is also a common-law misdemeanor. It would be punishable as a Class 1 misdemeanor under G.S. 14-3(a) (misdemeanors without specific classification and punishment).

Statute	Description of Offense	Punishment

Article 23: Trespasses to Personal Property

Statute	Description of Offense	Punishment
14-160(a)	Willful injury to personal property, causing damage up to $200	Class 2 misdemeanor
14-160(b)	Willful injury to personal property, causing more than $200 damage	Class 1 misdemeanor
14-160.1	Altering identification marks on personal property	Class 1 misdemeanor
14-163	Poisoning livestock	Class I felony
14-163.1	Injuring law-enforcement-agency animal	Class I felony[104]

Article 24: Vehicles and Draft Animals—Protection of Bailor against Acts of Bailee

Statute	Description of Offense	Punishment
14-165	Malicious injury to hired personal property	Class 2 misdemeanor
14-167	Failing to return hired property	Class 2 misdemeanor
14-168	Renting equipment or vehicle with intent to defraud	Class 2 misdemeanor
14-168.1	Conversion by bailee, lessee, tenant, or person with power of attorney:	
	if value of property is $400 or less	Class 1 misdemeanor
	if value of property exceeds $400	Class H felony
14-168.4	Failing to return rented equipment on which there is a purchase option, with intent to defeat owner's rights	Class 2 misdemeanor

Article 26: Offenses against Public Morality and Decency

Statute	Description of Offense	Punishment
14-177	Crime against nature	Class I felony
14-178	Incest between certain near relatives	Class F felony[105]
14-179	Incest between uncle and niece or aunt and nephew	Class 1 misdemeanor
14-183	Bigamy and bigamous cohabitation	Class I felony
14-184	Fornication and adultery	Class 2 misdemeanor
14-190.1	Disseminating obscenity	Class I felony
14-190.4	Coercing acceptance of obscene publication	Class 1 misdemeanor
14-190.5	Preparing obscene photograph, slide, or film for purpose of dissemination	Class 1 misdemeanor
14-190.6	Using child under 16 to assist in obscenity offense	Class I felony
14-190.7	Disseminating obscenity to child under 16	Class I felony
14-190.8	Disseminating obscenity to child under 13	Class I felony

104. For offenses committed on or after Oct. 1, 1994, and before Dec. 1, 1995, this offense was a Class 1 misdemeanor.

105. G.S. 14-178 defines near relatives as grandparent and grandchild, parent and child, parent and stepchild or legally adopted child, and brother and sister of the whole or half blood.

Statute	Description of Offense	Punishment
14-190.9	Indecent exposure or permitting use of premises for such	Class 2 misdemeanor
14-190.14	Displaying material harmful to minors	Class 2 misdemeanor[106]
14-190.15(a), -190.15(d)	Disseminating material harmful to minors	Class 1 misdemeanor
14-190.15(b), -190.15(d)	Exhibiting harmful performance to minor	Class 1 misdemeanor
14-190.16	First-degree sexual exploitation of minor	Class D felony[107]
14-190.17	Second-degree sexual exploitation of minor	Class F felony
14-190.17A	Third-degree sexual exploitation of minor	Class I felony
14-190.18	Promoting prostitution of minor	Class D felony[108]
14-190.19	Participating in prostitution of minor	Class F felony
14-196	Harassing phone calls	Class 2 misdemeanor
14-202	Peeping into room occupied by female	Class 1 misdemeanor
14-202.1	Taking, or attempting to take, indecent liberties with child	Class F felony
14-202.2	Indecent liberties between children	Class 1 misdemeanor[109]
14-202.3	Soliciting child by computer to commit unlawful sex act	Class I felony[110]

Article 26A: Adult Establishments[111]

Statute	Description of Offense	Punishment
14-202.11, -202.12	Permitting facility to contain multiple adult establishments:	
	First offense	Class 3 misdemeanor
	Subsequent offense	Class 2 misdemeanor
	Permitting adult establishment in facility where sexually oriented devices are contained:	
	First offense	Class 3 misdemeanor
	Subsequent offense	Class 2 misdemeanor

106. G.S. 14-190.14(b) provides that each day's violation is a separate offense.

107. For offenses committed on or after Oct. 1, 1994, and before Dec. 1, 1995, this offense was a Class E felony.

108. For offenses committed on or after Oct. 1, 1994, and before Dec. 1, 1995, this offense was a Class F felony.

109. This offense occurs when a person under 16 takes or attempts to take indecent liberties with a child who is at least 3 years younger than the person. Because the district court, in its capacity as juvenile court, has exclusive jurisdiction over a person who is under 16 and charged with a misdemeanor, G.S. 14-202.2 only provides the basis for a delinquency petition in juvenile court; the person may not be tried as an adult. G.S. 14-202.2 applies to offenses committed on or after Oct. 1, 1995.

110. G.S. 14-202.3 applies to offenses committed on or after Dec. 1, 1996.

111. Effective July 15, 1998, the definition of adult bookstore in G.S. 14-202.10(1) was broadened.

Statute	Description of Offense	Punishment
	Permitting multiple occupancy in viewing booth in adult mini–motion picture theater:	
	First offense	Class 3 misdemeanor
	Subsequent offense	Class 2 misdemeanor

Article 27: Prostitution[112]

Statute	Description of Offense	Punishment
14-204, -207, -208	Prostitution and aiding and abetting prostitution:	
	First-degree (two or more violations within 1 year preceding offense)	Class 1 misdemeanor[113]
	Second-degree	Class 1 misdemeanor
14-204.1	Loitering for purpose of prostitution	Class 1 misdemeanor

Article 27A: Sexual Offender Registration Program

Statute	Description of Offense	Punishment
14-208.11	Violating sex-offender registration requirements	Class F felony[114]

112. G.S. 14-208 provides that no female convicted under Article 27 may be placed on probation or parole in the care of any person except a female probation officer.

113. G.S. 14-208 provides that in the case of a commitment to a reformatory institution, the commitment shall be for an indeterminate period of not less than 1 nor more than 3 years. Under structured sentencing, however, such a lengthy period of confinement is not authorized for a Class 1 misdemeanor. Thus there no longer appears to be any special punishment for first-degree prostitution; the punishment is the same as for second-degree prostitution. *See* Thomas H. Thornburg, North Carolina Crimes: A Guidebook on the Elements of Crime 362 (4th ed. 1995).

114. The initial version of G.S. 14-208.11 applied to persons convicted or released from a penal institution on or after Jan. 1, 1996. A first violation of G.S. 14-208.11 was a Class 3 misdemeanor, and a subsequent violation was a Class I felony.

Effective for persons convicted or released from a penal institution on or after Apr. 3, 1997, the definition of "reportable conviction" in G.S. 14-208.6(4), which triggers the requirement to register, was revised slightly. *See also* G.S. 14-208.6(2) (effective same date, definition of "penal institution" revised).

Effective Apr. 1, 1998, a violation of G.S. 14-208.11 was made a Class F felony. Although not spelled out in the legislation, the increased punishment presumably applies only to violations committed on or after that date. *See generally* Lindh v. Murphy, 521 U.S. 320, 117 S. Ct. 2059, 138 L. Ed. 2d 481 (1997) (discussing general rules for interpreting statutes that would have retroactive effect); Landgraf v. USI Film Prods., 511 U.S. 244, 114 S. Ct. 1483, 128 L. Ed. 2d 229 (1994) (discussing similar principles). Also effective Apr. 1, 1998, the definition of "reportable conviction" was revised to add a new set of offenses involving minors. *See* G.S. 14-208.6(1d). As with earlier versions of the registration laws, this change may apply only to persons convicted or released on or after the stated effective date, but the legislation does not specify. Additional registration obligations for those required to register also were imposed, effective Apr. 1, 1998. *See, e.g.,* G.S. 14-208.9A.

Those classified as sexually violent predators are subject to stricter registration requirements. *See* G.S. 14-208.20 through -208.25 (effective date of Apr. 1, 1998, given without elaboration). A violation of these requirements is punishable under G.S. 14-208.11. Juveniles adjudicated delinquent of certain offenses also will be subject to registration requirements, effective Oct. 1, 1999. *See* G.S. 14-208.26 through -208.32. No criminal penalties are specified for a failure to comply; the court counselor assigned to the juvenile, and not the juvenile, is responsible for submitting the registration information.

Statute	Description of Offense	Punishment
Article 28: Perjury		
14-209	Perjury	Class F felony
14-210	Subornation of perjury	Class I felony
Article 29: Bribery		
14-217	Acceptance of bribe by public official	Class F felony
14-218	Offering a bribe	Class F felony
14-220	Offering bribe to, or acceptance of bribe by, juror	Class F felony
Article 30: Obstructing Justice[115]		
14-221	Breaking or entering jail, or conspiracy to break or enter jail, with intent to injure prisoner	Class F felony
14-221.1	Destruction of evidence	Class I felony
14-221.2	Altering court document or entering unauthorized judgment	Class H felony
14-223	Resisting, delaying, or obstructing officer	Class 2 misdemeanor
14-225	Making false report to law enforcement agency or officer	Class 2 misdemeanor
14-225.1	Picketing near courthouse with intent to interfere with administration of justice	Class 1 misdemeanor
14-225.2(a)(1), -225.2(c)	Harassing juror with intent to influence official action	Class H felony
14-225.2(a)(2), -225.2(c)	Harassing juror as result of prior official action	Class I felony
14-226	Intimidating, or attempting to intimidate, witness	Class H felony
14-226.1	Violating certain court orders	Class 3 misdemeanor[116]
Article 31: Misconduct in Public Office		
14-228	Buying or selling public office	Class I felony
14-230	Willful failure by public officer to discharge duties	Class 1 misdemeanor
14-234.1	Misuse of confidential information	Class 1 misdemeanor
14-239	Allowing prisoner to escape	Class 1 misdemeanor

115. Obstructing justice is also a common-law misdemeanor. It would be punishable as a Class 1 misdemeanor under G.S. 14-3(a) (misdemeanors without a specific classification and punishment) unless considered an "infamous" misdemeanor under G.S. 14-3(b), in which case it would be punishable as a Class H felony. *Compare* State v. Clemmons, 100 N.C. App. 286, 396 S.E.2d 616 (1990) (allegations of indictment were sufficient to raise offenses to felony) *with* State v. Preston, 73 N.C. App. 174, 325 S.E.2d 686 (1985) (allegations were insufficient to raise offense to felony).

116. G.S. 14-226.1 authorizes a fine up to $250.

Statute	Description of Offense	Punishment
14-242	Failing to return process or making false return	Class 1 misdemeanor
14-247, -251	Private use of public vehicle	Class 2 misdemeanor

Article 33: Prison Breach and Prisoners

Statute	Description of Offense	Punishment
14-255	Escape while hired out	Class 1 misdemeanor[117]
14-256	Escape from county or municipal facility or officer of such facility	Class 1 misdemeanor
14-256(1)	Escape from county or municipal facility by felon, pending transfer to state prison system	Class H felony[118]
14-256(2)	Escape from county or municipal facility by person serving sentence for felony	Class H felony[119]
14-256.1	Escape from private correctional facility in N.C. by person convicted in another jurisdiction	Class H felony[120]
14-258	Trading:[121]	
	with prisoners	Class H felony
	when article conveyed to prisoner leads to murder, assault, or escape	Class F felony
14-258.1(a)	Furnishing poison, narcotics, or weapon to inmate	Class H felony[122]
14-258.1(b)	Furnishing alcohol to inmate	Class 1 misdemeanor[123]
14-258.2(a)	Dangerous weapons in prison/jail:	
	Possession of dangerous weapon by inmate	Class H felony
	Assault with dangerous weapon, inflicting bodily injury	Class F felony
	Use of dangerous weapon to effect escape	Class F felony
14-258.2(b)	Use of dangerous weapon to assist escape by inmate	Class H felony
14-258.3	Taking of hostage by prisoner	Class F felony
14-259	Aiding escaped prisoner:	
	when prisoner is felon or charged with felony	Class I felony
	when prisoner is misdemeanant or charged with misdemeanor	Class 1 misdemeanor

117. For offenses committed on or after Oct. 1, 1994, and before Dec. 1, 1997, this offense was a Class 3 misdemeanor.

118. For offenses committed on or after Oct. 1, 1994, and before Dec. 1, 1997, this offense was a Class I felony.

119. *See* note 118.

120. G.S. 14-256.1 applies to offenses committed on or after Jan. 1, 1999.

121. G.S. 14-258 defines this offense as: (a) conveying messages to or from any convict; (b) conveying a weapon or instrument of escape to any prisoner; (c) trading with a convict for his or her clothing or for stolen goods; or (d) selling to a convict any article forbidden by prison rules.

122. G.S. 14-258.1 provides that if the defendant is employed by a state institution or local confinement facility, he or she shall be dismissed from employment.

123. *See* note 122.

Statute	Description of Offense	Punishment

Article 35: Offenses against the Public Peace[124]

Statute	Description of Offense	Punishment
14-269(a), -269(c)	Carrying concealed weapon	Class 2 misdemeanor
14-269(a1), -269(c)	Carrying concealed pistol or gun:[125]	
	First offense	Class 2 misdemeanor
	Subsequent offense	Class I felony
14-269.2(b)	Possession of certain firearms and explosives on educational property	Class I felony[126]
14-269.2(c)	Aiding a person under 18 to commit violation of 14-269.2(b)	Class I felony
14-269.2(d)	Possession of certain weapons, not specified in 14-269.2(c), on educational property	Class 1 misdemeanor
14-269.2(e)	Aiding a person under 18 to commit violation of 14-269.2(d)	Class 1 misdemeanor
14-269.3	Carrying gun into public event or establishment serving alcohol	Class 1 misdemeanor
14-269.4	Possession of weapon in courthouse and certain state property	Class 1 misdemeanor
14-269.6	Possession or sale of spring-loaded projectile knife	Class 1 misdemeanor
14-269.7	Possession of handgun by person under 18	Class 2 misdemeanor
14-269.8	Purchasing or attempting to purchase firearm while domestic violence protective order prohibits purchase	Class H felony[127]
14-275.1	Disorderly conduct at bus or railroad station or airport	Class 3 misdemeanor
14-276.1	Impersonation of firefighter or emergency medical personnel	Class 3 misdemeanor
14-277(a), -277(d1)(1)	Impersonation: falsely representing self as law-enforcement officer	Class 1 misdemeanor
14-277(a)(4), -277(d1)(3)	Impersonation: unlawfully operating vehicle with blue light	Class I felony[128]

124. Upon conviction of a violation of G.S. 14-269 (carrying concealed weapon), 14-269.7 (possession of handgun by minor), or any other offense involving use of a deadly weapon as defined in G.S. 14-269, the weapon is subject to confiscation and disposition as provided in G.S. 14-269.1.

125. G.S. 14-269(a1) applies to offenses committed on or after Dec. 1, 1995.

126. G.S. 14-269.2(f) provides that it is a Class 1 misdemeanor, not a Class I felony, to possess a firearm on educational property if (1) the person is not a student attending the school; (2) the firearm is not concealed; (3) the firearm is not loaded and is locked up; and (4) the person does not brandish, exhibit, or display the firearm in a callous, angry, or threatening manner.

127. G.S. 14-269.8 applies to offenses committed on or after Oct. 1, 1995.

128. For offenses committed on or after Oct. 1, 1994, and before Dec. 1, 1996, this offense was a Class 1 misdemeanor.

Statute	Description of Offense	Punishment
14-277(b), -277(d1)(2)	Impersonation: falsely representing self as law-enforcement officer and acting as such	Class 1 misdemeanor[129]
14-277(b)(5), -277(d1)(4)	Impersonation: unlawfully operating vehicle with blue light and causing reasonable person to yield or stop	Class H felony[130]
14-277(e)	Impersonation of city, county, or state employee	Class 1 misdemeanor
14-277.1	Communicating threats	Class 1 misdemeanor
14-277.2	Carrying weapon at parade or demonstration	Class 1 misdemeanor
14-277.3	Stalking:[131]	
	First offense	Class 1 misdemeanor
	While court order in effect prohibiting similar behavior	Class A1 misdemeanor
	Subsequent offense within 5 years	Class I felony
14-277.4(a), -277.4(c)	Obstructing health care facility:	
	First offense	Class 2 misdemeanor
	Second offense within 3 years	Class 1 misdemeanor
	Third or subsequent offense within 3 years	Class I felony
14-277.4(b), -277.4(c)	Injuring, or threatening to injure, person obtaining, aiding another to obtain, or providing health care services:	
	First offense	Class 2 misdemeanor
	Second offense within 3 years	Class 1 misdemeanor
	Third or subsequent offense within 3 years	Class I felony
14-277.4(d)	Violating injunction obtained pursuant to 14-277.4	Criminal contempt, punishable by less than 30 days or more than 1 year

Article 36: Offenses against the Public Safety

Statute	Description of Offense	Punishment
14-280	Shooting or throwing at train	Class I felony
14-281.1	Throwing object at sports event	Class 3 misdemeanor
14-283	Exploding dynamite cartridge or bomb	Class 1 misdemeanor
14-284	Unlicensed sale of explosives	Class 1 misdemeanor

129. Effective for offenses committed on or after Dec. 1, 1996, G.S. 14-277(d1)(2) provides that the court may impose an intermediate punishment for this offense even when structured sentencing authorizes a community punishment only.

130. For offenses committed on or after Oct. 1, 1994, and before Dec. 1, 1996, this offense was a Class 1 misdemeanor.

131. For offenses committed on or after Oct. 1, 1994, and before Dec. 1, 1997, a first offense was a Class 2 misdemeanor, and an offense committed while a court order was in effect prohibiting similar behavior was a Class 1 misdemeanor. In addition to the changes in punishment, the definition of stalking was rewritten for offenses committed on or after Dec. 1, 1997.

Statute	Description of Offense	Punishment
14-284.1	Violating regulations governing sale of explosives	Class 2 misdemeanor
14-284.2	Dumping toxic substances	Class F felony[132]
14-286	Giving false fire alarm	Class 2 misdemeanor
14-286.1	Making false ambulance request	Class 3 misdemeanor
14-286.2(a)(1)	Interfering with emergency radio communication, causing serious bodily injury or property damage in excess of $1,000	Class 1 misdemeanor
14-286.2(a)(2)	Interfering with emergency radio communication, not causing result in 14-286.2(a)(1)	Class 2 misdemeanor

Article 36A: Riots and Civil Disorders[133]

Statute	Description of Offense	Punishment
14-288.2(b)	Engaging in riot	Class 1 misdemeanor
14-288.2(c)(1)	Engaging in riot resulting in more than $1,500 property damage or serious bodily injury	Class H felony
14-288.2(c)(2)	Engaging in riot while possessing dangerous weapon or substance	Class H felony
14-288.2(d)	Inciting riot	Class 1 misdemeanor
14-288.2(e)	Inciting riot resulting in more than $1,500 property damage or serious bodily injury	Class F felony
14-288.4	Disorderly conduct	Class 2 misdemeanor
14-288.5	Failing to disperse when commanded	Class 2 misdemeanor
14-288.6(a)	Trespass during emergency	Class 1 misdemeanor
14-288.6(b)	Looting	Class H felony
14-288.7	Transporting dangerous weapon during emergency or riot	Class 1 misdemeanor
14-288.8	Manufacture, sale, possession, etc., of weapon of mass death and destruction	Class F felony
14-288.9	Assault on emergency personnel:	
	without dangerous weapon or substance	Class 1 misdemeanor
	with dangerous weapon or substance	Class F felony
14-288.12	Violating emergency proclamation issued pursuant to municipal ordinance	Class 3 misdemeanor[134]

132. G.S. 14-284.2 authorizes a fine up to $100,000 per day of violation.

133. The offenses of unlawful assembly and going armed to the terror of the people are common-law misdemeanors. Each would be punishable as a Class 1 misdemeanor under G.S. 14-3(a) (misdemeanors without specific classification and punishment). *Cf.* State v. Rambert, 341 N.C. 173, 459 S.E.2d 510 (1995) (offense of going armed to terror of people could not be elevated to felony because indictment did not allege that offense was "infamous" and thus did not put defendant on notice that he could be convicted of felony).

134. G.S. 14-4 contains general provisions on fines for ordinance violations. *See* note 10. Whether those provisions, or the structured sentencing rules for misdemeanors in G.S. 15A-1340.23(b), govern the fine for this offense is unclear.

Statute	Description of Offense	Punishment
14-288.13	Violating emergency proclamation issued pursuant to county ordinance	Class 3 misdemeanor[135]
14-288.14	Violating emergency proclamation where municipal proclamation extended to county	Class 3 misdemeanor
14-288.15	Violating emergency proclamation issued by governor	Class 2 misdemeanor
14-288.19	Violating governor's order to evacuate public building	Class 2 misdemeanor

Article 37: Lotteries, Gaming, Bingo, and Raffles[136]

Statute	Description of Offense	Punishment
14-290	Promoting or conducting unauthorized lottery	Class 2 misdemeanor[137]
14-291	Selling lottery tickets	Class 2 misdemeanor
14-291.1	Selling "numbers" tickets	Class 2 misdemeanor
14-291.2	Pyramid scheme:[138]	
	Establishing or operating	Class H felony[139]
	Participating in or otherwise promoting	Class 2 misdemeanor[140]
14-292	Gambling	Class 2 misdemeanor
14-293	Allowing gambling in houses of entertainment	Class 2 misdemeanor[141]
14-295	Gaming tables, illegal punchboards, and slot machines:	
	Keeping	Class 2 misdemeanor
	Playing	Class 2 misdemeanor
14-301, -303	Operating or possessing slot machine	Class 2 misdemeanor
14-302, -303	Operating or possessing gambling devices	Class 2 misdemeanor
14-304, -309	Manufacture, sale, etc., of slot machine	Class 2 misdemeanor
14-305, -309	Agreeing to provide thing of value to user of slot machine	Class 2 misdemeanor
14-309.20	Greyhound racing	Class 1 misdemeanor[142]

135. *See* note 134.

136. G.S. 14-299 provides for the seizure and sale or destruction of gambling equipment used in certain illegal operations.

137. G.S. 14-290 authorizes a fine of up to $2,000.

138. G.S. 14-291.2(c) provides that a superior court judge may, on petition of the attorney general or district attorney, enjoin the continuation of a pyramid scheme, assess civil penalties and attorneys' fees in such a proceeding, and appoint a receiver to secure assets obtained by the defendant through his or her participation in the scheme.

139. For offenses committed on or after Oct. 1, 1994, and before Dec. 1, 1997, this offense was a Class 2 misdemeanor.

140. G.S. 14-291.2(a) provides that any person who participates in or otherwise promotes a pyramid scheme "shall be deemed to have participated in a lottery."

141. G.S. 14-293 provides that any person convicted of this offense shall forfeit his or her license to do business and forever be barred from doing any of the businesses set out in the statute.

142. G.S. 14-309.20 applies to offenses committed on or after Jan. 1, 1999.

Article 39: Protection of Minors

Statute	Description of Offense	Punishment
14-313(b)	Sale of tobacco products or cigarette wrapping papers to person under 18:[143]	
	Selling or distributing to person under 18	Class 2 misdemeanor
	Purchasing on behalf of person under 18	Class 2 misdemeanor
	Failing to demand proof of age of person under 18	Class 2 misdemeanor
	Failing to post required notice	Infraction[144]
14-313(b1)	Unlawfully distributing tobacco products through vending machine	Class 2 misdemeanor[145]
14-313(c)	Purchase of tobacco products or cigarette wrapping papers by person under 18:[146]	
	Purchasing, receiving, or attempting to purchase or receive	Class 2 misdemeanor
	Presenting false proof of age	Class 2 misdemeanor
14-313(d)	Sending or assisting person under 18 to purchase or receive tobacco products or cigarette wrapping papers	Class 2 misdemeanor[147]
14-315(a)	Selling or giving weapon other than handgun to person under 18	Class 1 misdemeanor[148]
14-315(a1)	Selling or giving handgun to person under 18	Class H felony[149]
14-315.1	Storing firearm in manner accessible to minor	Class 1 misdemeanor
14-315.2(a), -315.2(c)	Failing to provide written copy of 14-315.1 to purchaser of firearm	Class 1 misdemeanor
14-315.2(b), -315.2(c)	Failing to post notice warning purchaser of duty to store firearm	Class 1 misdemeanor
14-316	Permitting child under 12 to use dangerous firearm	Class 2 misdemeanor
14-316.1	Contributing to delinquent, undisciplined, abused, or neglected condition of juvenile	Class 1 misdemeanor

143. G.S. 14-313(f) provides that any person charged with a misdemeanor shall be qualified for deferred prosecution if he or she has not previously been placed on probation for a violation of G.S. 14-313 and so states under oath. Effective for offenses committed on or after Dec. 1, 1995, the offenses in G.S. 14-313 were completely rewritten; effective for offenses committed on or after Dec. 1, 1997, further revisions were made and new offenses added.

144. G.S. 14-313(b) provides that a first offense is punishable by a $25 fine and a subsequent offense by a $75 fine.

145. *See* note 143.

146. *See* note 143. For offenses committed on or after Dec. 1, 1995, and before Dec. 1, 1997, this offense was an infraction, punishable under G.S. 14-3.1.

147. *See* note 143.

148. G.S. 14-315 provides that the defendant shall forfeit the proceeds of any sale.

149. *See* note 148. For offenses committed on or after Jan. 1, 1995, and before Jan. 1, 1997, this offense was a Class I felony. For offenses committed on or after Oct. 1, 1994, and before Jan. 1, 1995, this offense was a Class 1 misdemeanor, punishable under G.S. 14-315(a).

Statute	Description of Offense	Punishment
14-318.2	Misdemeanor child abuse	Class 1 misdemeanor[150]
14-318.4(a)	Intentionally inflicting serious injury on child	Class E felony
14-318.4(a1)	Committing, permitting, or encouraging prostitution by child	Class E felony
14-318.4(a2)	Parent or legal guardian committing or allowing commission of sexual act on child	Class E felony
14-320.1	Transporting child outside state with intent to violate custody order	Class I felony

Article 40: Protection of the Family

Statute	Description of Offense	Punishment
14-322(b), -322(f)	Abandonment of spouse without providing adequate support:[151]	
	First offense	Class 2 misdemeanor
	Subsequent offense	Class 1 misdemeanor
14-322(c), -322(f)	Failing to provide adequate support while living with dependent spouse:	
	First offense	Class 2 misdemeanor
	Subsequent offense	Class 1 misdemeanor
14-322(d), -322(f)	Nonsupport of child by parent:[152]	
	First offense	Class 2 misdemeanor
	Subsequent offense	Class 1 misdemeanor
14-322.1	Abandonment of child for 6 months and failure to support	Class I felony
14-326.1	Failing to support parent:	
	First offense	Class 2 misdemeanor
	Subsequent offense	Class 1 misdemeanor

Article 44: Regulation of Sales

Statute	Description of Offense	Punishment
14-344	Scalping tickets	Class 2 misdemeanor

150. The statute creates three separate offenses: (1) inflicting physical injury on a child; (2) allowing physical injury to be inflicted on a child; and (3) creating or allowing to be created a substantial risk of physical injury to a child. *See* State v. Fredell, 283 N.C. 242, 195 S.E.2d 300 (1973).

151. In addition to imposing the authorized punishment for this offense, the court is authorized to enter an order for support. *See* G.S. 14-322(e).

152. *See* note 151.

Article 47: Cruelty to Animals

Statute	Description of Offense	Punishment
14-360(a)	Intentional cruelty to animals	Class 1 misdemeanor[153]
14-360(b)	Malicious cruelty to animals	Class I felony[154]
14-361	Instigating or promoting cruelty to animals	Class 1 misdemeanor
14-361.1	Abandonment of animals without justifiable excuse	Class 2 misdemeanor
14-362	Cock fighting	Class 2 misdemeanor[155]
14-362.1(a)	Promoting fighting and baiting of animals other than cocks or dogs	Class 2 misdemeanor[156]
14-362.1(b)	Possession or training of animal other than cock or dog with intent to use in fighting exhibition	Class 2 misdemeanor
14-362.1(c)	Participating as spectator at animal fight other than cock or dog fight	Class 2 misdemeanor
14-362.1(d)	Promoting fighting and baiting of animals other than cocks or dogs within 3 years of prior conviction	Class I felony
14-362.2(a)	Promoting fighting or baiting of dog	Class H felony[157]
14-362.2(b)	Possession or training of dog with intent to use in fighting exhibition	Class H felony[158]
14-362.2(c)	Participating as spectator at dog fight	Class H felony[159]
14-363	Conveying animal in cruel manner	Class 1 misdemeanor

Article 52: Miscellaneous Police Regulations

Statute	Description of Offense	Punishment
14-394	Sending anonymous or threatening letters	Class 1 misdemeanor
14-395.1	Sexual harassment in leasing of property	Class 2 misdemeanor

153. Effective for offenses committed on or after Jan. 1, 1999, the definition of this offense was revised, but the punishment was not changed.

154. G.S. 14-360(b) applies to offenses committed on or after Jan. 1, 1999. It states that it does not increase the penalty for cock fighting provided in G.S. 14-362.

155. G.S. 14-362 provides that a lessor of property who knows that the property is used or intended to be used for fighting or baiting of an animal is under a duty to evict the lessee immediately.

156. G.S. 14-362.1(a) provides that a lessor of property who knows that the property is used or intended to be used for fighting or baiting of an animal is under a duty to evict the lessee immediately.

157. G.S. 14-362.2(a) provides that a lessor of property who knows that the property is used or intended to be used for fighting or baiting of an animal is under a duty to evict the lessee immediately. G.S. 14-362.2 applies to offenses committed on or after Dec. 1, 1997; before then, this offense was punishable under G.S. 14-362.1.

158. G.S. 14-362.2 applies to offenses committed on or after Dec. 1, 1997; before then, this offense was punishable under G.S. 14-362.1.

159. *See* note 158.

Statute	Description of Offense	Punishment
14-399(c)	Littering in an amount not more than 15 pounds and not for commercial purpose	Class 3 misdemeanor[160]
14-399(d)	Littering in an amount more than 15 but not exceeding 500 pounds and not for commercial purpose	Class 3 misdemeanor[161]
14-399(e)	Littering in an amount more than 500 pounds, or in any quantity for commercial purposes, or of hazardous waste	Class I felony[162]
14-401	Putting poisonous food or antifreeze in public place	Class 1 misdemeanor
14-401.6	Possession, use, or sale of tear gas	Class 2 misdemeanor
14-401.14(a)	Ethnic intimidation	Class 1 misdemeanor
14-401.14(b)	Teaching any technique to be used for ethnic intimidation	Class 1 misdemeanor
14-401.15	Telephone sales recovery services:[163]	
	engaging in	Class 1 misdemeanor
	collecting money for	Class H felony
14-401.16(a), -401.16(c)	Contaminating food or drink to render person incapacitated or helpless	Class H felony[164]
14-401.16(b), -401.16(c)	Manufacture, sale, or delivery of controlled substance, or possession with intent to manufacture, sell, or deliver, for purpose of violating 14-401.16(a)	Class H felony[165]

160. G.S. 14-399(c) provides that the punishment for a first offense is a fine from $100 to $500 and that the punishment for a subsequent offense within 3 years of a prior littering offense is a fine from $100 to $1,000. Active imprisonment is not authorized, but the court may require 8 to 24 hours of community service for a first offense and 16 to 50 hours for a subsequent offense within 3 years of a prior littering offense. Any community service shall consist of picking up litter or other labor commensurate with the offense. (The community service ranges apply to offenses committed on or after Dec. 1, 1997.) G.S. 14-399(f1) provides that a person who is found guilty of any littering offense while operating a motor vehicle shall receive 1 driver's license point under G.S. 20-16(c).

161. G.S. 14-399(d) provides that the punishment is a fine from $100 to $1,000. Active imprisonment is not authorized, but the court shall require 24 to 100 hours of community service consisting of picking up litter or other labor commensurate with the offense. (The community service range applies to offenses committed on or after Dec. 1, 1997.) G.S. 14-399(f1) provides that a person who is found guilty of any littering offense while operating a motor vehicle shall receive 1 driver's license point under G.S. 20-16(c).

162. G.S. 14-399(e) provides that the court may order the violator to remove the litter or render it harmless, repair or restore damaged property, pay damages, or perform community service. G.S. 14-399(g) provides that a motor vehicle, vessel, etc., involved in the disposal of more than 500 pounds of litter is subject to forfeiture. G.S. 14-399(f1) provides that a person who commits any littering offense while operating a motor vehicle shall receive 1 driver's license point under G.S. 20-16(c).

163. G.S. 14-401.15 applies to offenses committed on or after Jan. 1, 1998.

164. G.S. 14-401.16(c) makes this offense a Class G felony if the person acted with the intent of committing an offense under G.S. 14-27.3 (second-degree rape) or G.S. 14-27.5 (second-degree sex offense). G.S. 14-401.16 applies to offenses committed on or after Dec. 1, 1997.

165. *See* note 164.

Statute	Description of Offense	Punishment
Article 52A: Sale of Weapons in Certain Counties		
14-409	Sale or possession of machine gun	Class I felony
Article 54: Sale, etc., of Pyrotechnics		
14-410(a), -415	Making, selling, or using certain fireworks	Class 2 misdemeanor
14-410(b), -415	Selling certain pyrotechnics to person under 16	Class 2 misdemeanor[166]
Article 54A: Felony Firearms Act		
14-415.1	Possession of certain firearms by felon	Class G felony[167]
14-415.3	Possession of firearm by person acquitted by reason of insanity or found incompetent to proceed	Class H felony
Article 54B: Concealed Handgun Permit		
14-415.21, -3.1	Carrying concealed handgun after having been issued valid permit and failing to carry permit or failing to make required disclosures to law-enforcement officer:[168]	
	First offense	Infraction[169]
	Subsequent offense	Class 2 misdemeanor
Article 59: Public Intoxication		
14-444	Intoxicated and disruptive in public	Class 3 misdemeanor[170]
Article 60: Computer-related Crime		
14-454(a)	Accessing of computer for certain purposes:[171]	
	when loss or damage exceeds $1,000	Class G felony
	when loss or damage is $1,000 or less	Class 1 misdemeanor

166. G.S. 14-410(b) applies to offenses committed on or after Dec. 1, 1995.

167. Effective for offenses committed on or after Dec. 1, 1995, G.S. 14-415.1 was revised as follows: the offense was changed from a Class H to a Class G felony; the 5-year ban was changed to a lifetime ban on possession of certain firearms by a felon outside the home or business; and the types of felony convictions resulting in such a ban were expanded to include all felony convictions occurring before, on, or after Dec. 1, 1995.

168. G.S. 14-415.21 applies to offenses committed on or after Dec. 1, 1995.

169. In lieu of paying a fine for a first offense, the person may surrender the handgun permit.

170. G.S. 14-444(b) provides that a magistrate may not accept a guilty plea and enter judgment for this offense, despite the provisions of G.S. 7A-273(1).

171. For offenses committed on or after Oct. 1, 1994, and before Dec. 1, 1994, this offense was a Class H felony regardless of the amount of the loss or damage.

Statute	Description of Offense	Punishment
14-454(b)	Unauthorized accessing of computer for purpose other than set forth in 14-454(a)	Class 1 misdemeanor
14-455(a)	Damaging computer:[172]	
	when damage exceeds $1,000	Class G felony
	when damage is $1,000 or less	Class 1 misdemeanor
14-456	Denying computer services to authorized user	Class 1 misdemeanor
14-457	Threatening to damage computer or computer program with intent to extort	Class H felony

Article 61: Trains and Railroads

Statute	Description of Offense	Punishment
14-460	Riding on train unlawfully	Class 3 misdemeanor[173]
14-461	Unauthorized manufacture or sale of switch-lock keys	Class 1 misdemeanor[174]

Chapter 15A: Criminal Procedure Act

Article 16: Electronic Surveillance[175]

Statute	Description of Offense	Punishment
15A-287(a)(1)	Unauthorized interception of communication	Class H felony
15A-287(a)(2)	Unauthorized use of device to intercept oral communication	Class H felony
15A-287(a)(3)	Disclosure of unlawfully-intercepted communication	Class H felony

Article 26: Bail

Statute	Description of Offense	Punishment
15A-543(b)(1)	Failing to appear after release in connection with felony	Class I felony
15A-543(b)(2)	Failing to appear after release following conviction in superior court	Class I felony
15A-543(c)	Failing to appear after release in connection with misdemeanor	Class 2 misdemeanor

172. *See* note 171.

173. G.S. 14-460 applies to offenses committed on or after Sept. 4, 1998. G.S. 62-319 contains the same prohibition and applies to offenses committed before or after that date.

174. G.S. 14-461 applies to offenses committed on or after Sept. 4, 1998. G.S. 62-322 contains the same prohibition and applies to offenses committed before or after that date.

175. G.S. 15A-287(g) provides that a public officer who violates G.S. 15A-287(a) shall be removed from and shall be ineligible to hold any public office, elective or appointed. G.S. 15A-287 applies to offenses committed on or after Dec. 1, 1995.

Chapter 18B: Regulation of Alcoholic Beverages[176]

Statute	Description of Offense	Punishment
18B-102	Manufacture, sale, transport, import, export, delivery, furnishing, purchase, consumption, or possession of alcoholic beverages except as authorized by Ch. 18B	Class 1 misdemeanor
18B-111, -102(b)	Possession, transportation, or sale of nontaxpaid alcoholic beverage	Class 1 misdemeanor
18B-300(b), -102(b)	Consumption of wine or beer on premises having only off-premises permit	Class 1 misdemeanor
18B-301(f)(1)c, -102(b)	Consumption of fortified wine, spirituous liquor, or mixed beverage on public road or sidewalk	Class 1 misdemeanor
18B-301(f)(2), -102(b)	Displaying fortified wine, spirituous liquor, or mixed beverage at athletic contest	Class 1 misdemeanor
18B-301(f)(4), -102(b)	Possession or consumption of fortified wine, spirituous liquor, or mixed beverage on unauthorized premises	Class 1 misdemeanor
18B-301(f)(7), -102(b)	Possession or consumption of beer or wine on school property of local board of education	Class 1 misdemeanor
18B-302(a), -102(b)	Sale of alcoholic beverage to person under 21	Class 1 misdemeanor
18B-302(b)(1), -302(i), -102(b)	Purchase, attempted purchase, or possession of beer or unfortified wine:	
	by person 19 or 20 years old	Infraction, punishable by fine up to $25[177]
	by person under 19	Class 1 misdemeanor
18B-302(b)(2), -102(b)	Purchase, attempted purchase, or possession of fortified wine, spirituous liquor, or mixed beverage by person under 21	Class 1 misdemeanor
18B-302(c)	Aiding violation of 18B-302(a) or (b):	
	if aider is under 21	Class 2 misdemeanor
	if aider is 21 or older	Class 1 misdemeanor
18B-302(e), -102(b)	Fraudulent use of identification to obtain or attempt to obtain alcoholic beverage	Class 1 misdemeanor

176. G.S. 18B-101(4) defines an "alcoholic beverage" as a beverage containing at least 0.5 percent alcohol by volume, including malt beverages, unfortified wine, spirituous liquor, and mixed beverages. G.S. 18B-102(b) provides that a violation of Chapter 18B is a Class 1 misdemeanor "[u]nless a different punishment is otherwise expressly stated." In addition to any fine and sentence of imprisonment, G.S. 18B-102(b) provides that the court may impose the provisions of G.S. 18B-202 (removal from office or discharge from employment of any commission or local board member or employee or ALE agent convicted of violation of Chapter 18B), 18B-503 (sale or destruction of seized beverages), 18B-504 (forfeiture of property connected to offense), and 18B-505 (restitution to law enforcement agency for expenses incurred in purchasing beverages as part of investigation). G.S. 18B-104 authorizes certain administrative penalties for violation of the alcoholic beverage control [ABC] laws by a permittee.

177. Court costs may not be assessed in connection with this infraction. *See* G.S. 18B-302(i).

Statute	Description of Offense	Punishment
18B-302(f), -102(b)	Allowing use of identification by person who violates or attempts to violate 18B-302(b)	Class 1 misdemeanor
18B-303, -403, -102(b)	Purchase or sale of alcoholic beverage in amount greater than authorized by statute	Class 1 misdemeanor
18B-304, -102(b)	Sale of alcoholic beverage without permit	Class 1 misdemeanor
18B-307(b), -307(c), -102(b)	Manufacture of alcoholic beverage without permit:	
	First offense	Class 1 misdemeanor
	Subsequent offense	Class I felony
18B-401(a)	Transportation of alcoholic beverage:	
	Transportation of open bottle of fortified wine or spirituous liquor in passenger area	Class 3 misdemeanor
	Consumption of beer or wine by driver of motor vehicle	Class 3 misdemeanor
18B-406, -102(b)	Transportation of unauthorized amount of alcoholic beverage	Class 1 misdemeanor
18B-702(f)	Embezzlement by employee of local ABC Board	Class H felony
18B-1004, -102(b)	Selling or consuming alcoholic beverage after hours on licensed premises	Class 1 misdemeanor

Chapter 20: Motor Vehicles[178]

Statute	Description of Offense	Punishment
20-106	Receiving, transferring, or possessing stolen vehicle	Class H felony[179]
20-141.4(a1), -141.4(b)	Felony death by vehicle	Class G felony
20-141.4(a2), -141.4(b)	Misdemeanor death by vehicle	Class 1 misdemeanor
20-174.1	Sitting, standing, or lying on highway or street	Class 2 misdemeanor

Chapter 49: Bastardy

Statute	Description of Offense	Punishment
49-2, -8	Nonsupport of illegitimate child by parent	Class 2 misdemeanor[180]

Chapter 50B: Domestic Violence

Statute	Description of Offense	Punishment
50B-4.1	Knowingly violating valid protective order	Class A1 misdemeanor[181]

178. A more complete listing of motor vehicle offenses is contained in the "Punishment Chart for North Carolina Motor Vehicle Offenses," which appears in Part 2 of this book.

179. Conveyances used to conceal, convey, or transport property in violation of G.S. 20-106 are subject to forfeiture as provided in G.S. 14-86.1.

180. G.S. 49-8 also authorizes the following dispositions: (1) suspension of sentence and continuance; (2) probation, conditioned on payment of support; (3) order to pay mother's medical expenses; and (4) order to sign recognizance for compliance with court order.

181. G.S. 50B-4.1 applies to offenses committed on or after Dec. 1, 1997.

Statute	Description of Offense	Punishment
Chapter 53: Banks		
53-129	Embezzlement by bank officer or employee:	
	of less than $100,000	Class H felony
	of $100,000 or more	Class C felony[182]
53-276, -287	Engaging in check cashing business without license	Class I felony[183]
Chapter 58: Insurance		
58-2-161	False statement in support of or in opposition to claim for insurance benefits	Class H felony[184]
58-2-162	Embezzlement by insurance agent:	
	of things valued less than $100,000	Class H felony
	of things valued $100,000 or more	Class C felony[185]
Chapter 62: Public Utilities		
62-150	Entering conveyance by intoxicated person after being forbidden by driver	Class 1 misdemeanor
Chapter 62A: Public Safety Telephone Service		
62A-12	Misusing 911 system	Class 1 misdemeanor
Chapter 63: Aeronautics		
63-26.1	Trespassing on airport property	Class 2 misdemeanor
63-37.1	Obstructing takeoff or landing of aircraft at airport	Class 1 misdemeanor[186]
Chapter 67: Dogs		
67-4.2(a)(1), -4.2(c)	Leaving dangerous dog unrestrained on owner's property	Class 3 misdemeanor

182. For offenses committed on or after Oct. 1, 1994, and before Dec. 1, 1997, this offense was a class H felony.

183. G.S. 53-287 states that each transaction involving the unlawful cashing of a check, draft, or money order constitutes a separate offense. G.S. 53-276 and -287 apply to offenses committed on or after Oct. 1, 1997.

184. Effective for offenses committed on or after Oct. 1, 1995, G.S. 58-2-161 was revised as follows: the definition of the offense was rewritten; the offense was changed from a Class I to a Class H felony; and conspiracy or solicitation to present a fraudulent statement was made a Class H felony. The revised statute also allows the court to order as a condition of probation that the defendant pay restitution; in determining the amount of restitution, the reasonable costs and attorneys' fees incurred by the victim in investigating the claim may be considered part of the damage arising out of the offense.

185. For offenses committed on or after Oct. 1, 1994, and before Dec. 1, 1997, this offense was a Class H felony.

186. G.S. 63-37.1 applies to offenses committed on or after Dec. 1, 1995.

Statute	Description of Offense	Punishment
67-4.2(a)(2), -4.2(c)	Permitting dangerous dog to go unrestrained beyond owner's property	Class 3 misdemeanor
67-4.3	Owning dangerous dog that attacks person and causes physical injury requiring medical treatment in excess of $100	Class 1 misdemeanor
67-12	Permitting dog to run at large at night	Class 3 misdemeanor

Chapter 90: Medicine and Allied Occupations

Article 5: North Carolina Controlled Substances Act[187]

Statute	Description of Offense	Punishment
90-95(a)(1), -95(b)(1)	Schedule I or II controlled substance:	
	Sale	Class G felony[188]
	Manufacture, delivery, or possession with intent to manufacture, sell, or deliver	Class H felony

187. G.S. 90-96(a) contains special provisions for sentencing first-time offenders found guilty of misdemeanor possession of a Schedule II through VI controlled substance and first-time offenders found guilty of possessing less than 1 gram of cocaine. G.S. 90-96(a1) contains special provisions for sentencing first-time offenders convicted of any offense included in G.S. 90-95(a)(3).

Several other statutory provisions apply to any violation of the Controlled Substances Act:

A. G.S. 90-95(e) provides for increased punishment for any violation of the Act as follows:
   1. If the offense is a Class 1 misdemeanor and the defendant has previously been convicted under state or federal law of an offense punishable under the Act, the defendant shall be punished as a Class I felon. If the offense is a Class 2 misdemeanor and the defendant has a prior conviction as set out above, the defendant is guilty of a Class 1 misdemeanor. If the offense requires a suspended sentence and the defendant has a prior conviction as set out above, he or she is guilty of a Class 2 misdemeanor.
   2. For the purpose of increasing punishment, prior convictions are counted by the number of separate trials at which final convictions were obtained, not by the number of charges at a single trial.
   3. A prior conviction used to raise an offense to a higher class may not be used to calculate prior record or conviction level.

B. G.S. 90-95(f) provides that a person convicted of an offense under the Act who is sentenced to an active term of imprisonment less than the maximum term that could have been imposed may also be sentenced to post-prison probation to follow the active sentence for a period up to 5 years. Upon revocation of this probation, the original term of imprisonment may be increased by no more than the difference between the active term of imprisonment served and the maximum active term that could have been imposed.

C. G.S. 90-95.3 authorizes the court to order a person convicted of a violation of the Act to make restitution to any law-enforcement agency for reasonable expenditures made in buying controlled substances from the defendant, and to the State of North Carolina in the amount of $100 for the expense of analyzing any controlled substance, when such expenses were incurred as part of an investigation leading to the defendant's conviction.

D. Property used in connection with a violation of the Act is subject to forfeiture as provided in G.S. 90-112 and -112.1.

188. For offenses committed on or after Oct. 1, 1994, and before Dec. 1, 1997, a sale in violation of G.S. 90-95(a)(1) was the same class of offense as delivery. The change in punishment does not appear to affect the rule that sale and delivery of the same controlled substance is one offense, subject to one punishment. *See* State v. Moore, 327 N.C. 378, 395 S.E.2d 124 (1990).

Statute	Description of Offense	Punishment
90-95(a)(1), -95(b)(2)	Schedule III–VI controlled substance:	
	Sale	Class H felony[189]
	Manufacture, delivery, or possession with intent to manufacture, sell, or deliver	Class I felony[190]
90-95(a)(2), -95(c)	Counterfeit controlled substance: creation, sale, delivery, or possession with intent to sell or deliver	Class I felony
90-95(a)(3), -95(d)(1)	Possession of Schedule I controlled substance	Class I felony
90-95(a)(3), -95(d)(2)	Possession of Schedule II–IV controlled substance:	
	100 dosage units or less, except cocaine, PCP, or hydromorphone	Class 1 misdemeanor
	any quantity of cocaine or PCP, more than 4 dosage units of hydromorphone, or more than 100 dosage units of other substances	Class I felony
90-95(a)(3), -95(d)(3)	Possession of Schedule V controlled substance	Class 2 misdemeanor
90-95(a)(3), -95(d)(4)	Possession of Schedule VI controlled substance:	
	up to ½ oz. marijuana or $\frac{1}{20}$ oz. hashish	Class 3 misdemeanor[191]
	more than ½ oz. marijuana or $\frac{1}{20}$ oz. hashish	Class 1 misdemeanor
	more than 1½ oz. marijuana or $\frac{3}{20}$ oz. hashish or other specified synthetic substance	Class I felony
90-95(d1)(1)	Precursor chemicals: possession with intent to manufacture controlled substance	Class H felony
90-95(d1)(2)	Precursor chemicals: possession or distribution with knowledge that precursor chemical will be used to manufacture controlled substance	Class H felony
90-95(e)(5), -95(a)(1)	Sale or delivery of controlled substance in violation of 90-95(a)(1):[192]	
	by person 18 or older to person under 16 but over 13 or to pregnant female	Class D felony
	by person 18 or older to person 13 or younger	Class C felony

189. *See* note 188.

190. G.S. 90-95(b)(2) provides that the transfer of less than 5 grams of marijuana for no remuneration does not constitute a delivery in violation of G.S. 90-95(a)(1).

191. Any sentence of imprisonment must be suspended, and the sentencing judge may not impose a period of imprisonment as a special condition of probation. *See* G.S. 90-95(d)(4).

192. G.S. 90-95(e)(5) does not specifically address the consequences of transferring less than 5 grams of marijuana for no remuneration. *Compare* G.S. 90-95(e)(8) (stating that such a transfer does not constitute a delivery in violation of G.S. 90-95(a)(1)). Because a sale or delivery in violation of G.S. 90-95(a)(1) is a required element of this offense, however, such a transfer may not constitute a violation of G.S. 90-95(e)(5). *See* G.S. 90-95(b)(2) (also stating that such a transfer does not constitute a delivery in violation of G.S. 90-95(a)(1)).

For offenses committed on or after Jan. 1, 1997, but before Jan. 1, 1999, a violation of G.S. 90-95(e)(5) involving a minor was a Class D felony regardless of whether the minor was under 16 or 13. For offenses committed on or after Oct. 1, 1994, and before Jan. 1, 1997, a violation involving a minor or a pregnant female was a Class E felony.

Statute	Description of Offense	Punishment
90-95(e)(8), -95(a)(1)	Violation of 90-95(a)(1) by person 21 or older within 300 feet of elementary or secondary school	Class E felony[193]
90-95(e)(9), -95(a)(3)	Possession of controlled substance in prison or jail	Class H felony[194]
90-95(h)(1)	Trafficking in marijuana:[195]	
	more than 10 and less than 50 pounds	Class H drug-trafficking felony; fine of not less than $5,000[196]
	50–1,999 pounds	Class G drug-trafficking felony; fine of not less than $25,000[197]
	2,000–9,999 pounds	Class F drug-trafficking felony; fine of not less than $50,000
	10,000 pounds or more	Class D drug-trafficking felony; fine of not less than $200,000

193. G.S. 90-95(e)(8) provides that the transfer of less than 5 grams of marijuana for no remuneration does not constitute a delivery in violation of G.S. 90-95(a)(1).

194. For offenses committed on or after Oct. 1, 1994, and before Dec. 1, 1997, this offense was a Class I felony.

195. Individuals convicted of drug trafficking are not sentenced according to the usual structured sentencing rules. A person convicted of drug trafficking must receive the fine set forth in the text and the following minimum and maximum sentence regardless of the person's prior record level:

Class C drug-trafficking felony: Minimum 225 months; maximum 279 months.
Class D drug-trafficking felony: Minimum 175 months; maximum 219 months.
Class E drug-trafficking felony: Minimum 90 months; maximum 117 months.
Class F drug-trafficking felony: Minimum 70 months; maximum 84 months.
Class G drug-trafficking felony: Minimum 35 months; maximum 42 months.
Class H drug-trafficking felony: Minimum 25 months; maximum 30 months.

G.S. 90-95(h)(5) provides that the court may reduce the fine, impose a prison term less than the applicable minimum, or suspend the prison term and place the person on probation upon a finding that the person provided "substantial assistance" in the prosecution of others involved. *See also* State v. Saunders, 131 N.C. __, 507 S.E.2d 911 (1998) (in imposing sentence after finding substantial assistance, court is not required to impose minimum sentence prescribed under structured sentencing). G.S. 90-95(h)(6) provides that sentences imposed under G.S. 90-95(h) must run consecutively with, and begin at the expiration of, any other sentences being served by the defendant. When two or more offenses are being disposed of in the same proceeding, however, the court apparently is not required to impose consecutive sentences. *See* State v. Thomas, 85 N.C. App. 319, 354 S.E.2d 891 (1987) (construing similar consecutive sentencing provisions); State v. Crain, 73 N.C. App. 269, 326 S.E.2d 120 (1985) (to same effect).

196. For offenses committed on or after Oct. 1, 1994, and before Dec. 1, 1997, the amount of marijuana required for conviction of this class of offense was 50 to 99 pounds.

197. For offenses committed on or after Oct. 1, 1994, and before Dec. 1, 1997, the amount of marijuana required for conviction of this class of offense was 100 to 1,999 pounds.

Statute	Description of Offense	Punishment
90-95(h)(2)	Trafficking in methaqualone:[198]	
	1,000–4,999 dosage units	Class G drug-trafficking felony; fine of not less than $25,000
	5,000–9,999 dosage units	Class F drug-trafficking felony; fine of not less than $50,000
	10,000 dosage units or more	Class D drug-trafficking felony; fine of not less than $200,000
90-95(h)(3)	Trafficking in cocaine:[199]	
	28–199 grams	Class G drug-trafficking felony; fine of not less than $50,000
	200–399 grams	Class F drug-trafficking felony; fine of not less than $100,000
	400 grams or more	Class D drug-trafficking felony; fine of not less than $250,000
90-95(h)(3a)	Trafficking in amphetamine:[200]	
	1,000–4,999 dosage units	Class G drug-trafficking felony; fine of not less than $25,000
	5,000–9,999 dosage units	Class F drug-trafficking felony; fine of not less than $50,000
	10,000 dosage units or more	Class D drug-trafficking felony; fine of not less than $200,000
90-95(h)(3b)	Trafficking in methamphetamine:[201]	
	28–199 grams	Class G drug-trafficking felony; fine of not less than $50,000
	200–399 grams	Class F drug-trafficking felony; fine of not less than $100,000
	400 grams or more	Class D drug-trafficking felony; fine of not less than $250,000
90-95(h)(4)	Trafficking in opium or heroin:[202]	
	4–13 grams	Class F drug-trafficking felony; fine of not less than $50,000
	14–27 grams	Class E drug-trafficking felony; fine of not less than $100,000
	28 grams or more	Class C drug-trafficking felony; fine of not less than $500,000

198. *See* note 195.

199. *See* note 195.

200. *See* note 195.

201. *See* note 195.

202. *See* note 195.

Statute	Description of Offense	Punishment
90-95(h)(4a)	Trafficking in LSD:[203]	
	100–499 dosage units	Class G drug-trafficking felony; fine of not less than $25,000
	500–999 dosage units	Class F drug-trafficking felony; fine of not less than $50,000
	1,000 dosage units or more	Class D drug-trafficking felony; fine of not less than $200,000
90-95(i)	Conspiracy to commit drug-trafficking offense	Punishable by same penalties as for drug-trafficking felony defendant conspired to commit[204]
90-95.1	Continuing criminal enterprise	Class C felony; forfeiture of enterprise profits and other property set out in statute
90-95.4(a), -95(a)(1)	Hiring or intentionally using minor to violate 90-95(a)(1):[205]	
	when defendant is at least 18 but less than 21 and minor is more than 13	Felony one class greater than violation for which minor was hired
	when defendant is at least 18 but less than 21 and minor is 13 or younger	Felony two classes greater than violation for which minor was hired
90-95.4(b), -95(a)(1)	Hiring or intentionally using minor to violate 90-95(a)(1):[206]	
	when defendant is 21 or older and minor is more than 13	Felony three classes greater than violation for which minor was hired
	when defendant is 21 or older and minor is 13 or younger	Felony four classes greater than violation for which minor was hired

203. *See* note 195.

204. Under G.S. 90-95(i), a drug-trafficking conspiracy is the same class of offense as a completed drug-trafficking offense and is subject to the same mandatory minimum penalties and exceptions. *See* note 195. But a drug-trafficking conspiracy is subject to a limitation not applicable to a completed trafficking offense. In *State v. Worthington,* 84 N.C. App. 150, 352 S.E.2d 695 (1987), the court held that a defendant may not be convicted of both a trafficking conspiracy to possess a controlled substance and a trafficking conspiracy to sell a controlled substance when the evidence shows only *one* agreement, even though the agreement involves more than one substantive offense. *Compare* State v. Perry, 316 N.C. 87, 340 S.E.2d 450 (1986) (approving separate charges and convictions for trafficking by possession, trafficking by manufacturing, and trafficking by transporting, even when the same contraband material is used in each offense).

205. For offenses committed on or after Oct. 1, 1994, and before Jan. 1, 1999, a violation of G.S. 90-95.4(a) was a felony one class greater than the violation for which the minor was hired regardless of the age of the minor. Additionally, the defendant must have hired the minor, not hired *or* intentionally used the minor as under the current statute.

206. For offenses committed on or after Oct. 1, 1994, and before Jan. 1, 1999, a violation of G.S. 90-95.4(b) was a felony two classes greater than the violation for which the minor was hired regardless of the age of the minor. Additionally, the defendant must have hired the minor, not hired *or* intentionally used the minor as under the current statute.

Statute	Description of Offense	Punishment
90-95.6, -95(a)(1)	Promotion by person 21 or older of violation of 90-95(a)(1) by minor	Class D felony[207]
90-95.7, -95(a)(1)	Purchasing or receiving controlled substance by person 21 or older from minor 13 or younger who violates 90-95(a)(1)	Class G felony[208]
90-98	Controlled Substances Act:	
	Conspiracy to violate	Same class as offense for which conspiracy created
	Attempt to violate	Same class as offense attempted[209]
90-108(a)(1)	Impersonating a licensed practitioner	Class 1 misdemeanor[210]
90-108(a)(2)	Unlawful distribution by registrant or practitioner	Class 1 misdemeanor[211]
90-108(a)(3), -108(a)(8), -108(a)(9)	Violating registration provisions relating to authorized manufacture or distribution	Class 1 misdemeanor[212]
90-108(a)(5)	Failing to keep or furnish records required by Act	Class 1 misdemeanor[213]
90-108(a)(7)	Maintaining building or vehicle for use by persons violating Act, or for keeping or selling controlled substance	Class 1 misdemeanor[214]
90-108(a)(7), -108(b)	Violating 90-108(a)(7) while fortifying structure with intent to impede law enforcement entry	Class I felony
90-108(a)(10)	Obtaining controlled substance by fraud or deception	Class I felony[215]

207. G.S. 90-95.6 applies to offenses committed on or after Jan. 1, 1999.

208. G.S. 90-95.7 applies to offenses committed on or after Jan. 1, 1999.

209. Under G.S. 90-98 an attempt to commit a drug-trafficking offense is the same class of offense as the completed offense, but it is subject to the regular structured-sentencing punishments; the mandatory minimum penalties for a completed drug-trafficking offense are not applicable to an attempt. *Compare* G.S. 90-95(i) (prescribing mandatory minimum penalties for drug-trafficking offense and conspiracy to commit drug-trafficking offense but not for attempt to commit drug-trafficking offense).

210. G.S. 90-108(b) provides that "if the criminal pleading alleges that the violation was committed intentionally, and upon trial it is specifically found that the violation was committed intentionally, such violations shall be a Class I felony."

211. *See* note 210.

212. *See* note 210.

213. *See* note 210.

214. In State v. Bright, 78 N.C. App. 239, 337 S.E.2d 87 (1985), the court considered the applicability of G.S. 90-108(b) to this offense. *See* note 210. The court held that maintaining a vehicle with knowledge that it is used in connection with controlled substances is a misdemeanor, while maintaining a vehicle with *intent* that it be so used is a Class I felony.

215. The court of appeals has held that, because any commission of this offense is by definition intentional and because G.S. 90-108(b) provides that an intentional violation of G.S. 90-108 is a Class I felony, a misdemeanor offense under G.S. 90-108(a)(10) does not exist. *See* State v. Church, 73 N.C. App. 645, 327 S.E.2d 33 (1985); *but cf.* Ratzlaf v. United States, 510 U.S. 135, 114 S. Ct. 655, 126 L. Ed. 2d 615 (1994) (where willful violation of statute was required for conviction, government had to prove defendant acted with knowledge of illegality of conduct).

Statute	Description of Offense	Punishment
90-108(a)(13)	Obtaining controlled substance by use of legal prescription obtained by misrepresentation	Class 1 misdemeanor[216]
90-108(a)(14)	Embezzlement of controlled substance by employee of registrant or practitioner	Class 1 misdemeanor[217]

Article 5A: North Carolina Toxic Vapors Act[218]

Statute	Description of Offense	Punishment
90-113.10, -113.13	Inhaling fumes for purpose of intoxication	Class 1 misdemeanor
90-113.11, -113.13	Possession of substance for purpose of inhaling for intoxication	Class 1 misdemeanor
90-113.12, -113.13	Sale of substance with knowledge of intended illegal use	Class 1 misdemeanor

Article 5B: Drug Paraphernalia[219]

Statute	Description of Offense	Punishment
90-113.22	Possession of paraphernalia	Class 1 misdemeanor
90-113.23	Delivery, possession with intent to deliver, or manufacture with intent to deliver	Class 1 misdemeanor
90-113.23(c)	Delivery by person over 18 to minor at least 3 years younger	Class I felony
90-113.24	Advertisement of paraphernalia	Class 2 misdemeanor

Chapter 96: Employment Security

Statute	Description of Offense	Punishment
96-18(a)	False statement to obtain benefit	Class 1 misdemeanor
96-18(b)	Violations by employer:	
	False statement to avoid or reduce benefit or contribution	Class 1 misdemeanor
	Failing to produce required records	Class 1 misdemeanor
96-18(c)	Other violations of employment security laws	Class 1 misdemeanor

216. *See* note 210.

217. *See* note 210.

218. G.S. 90-113.14(a) and (a1) contain special provisions for sentencing first-time offenders who violate G.S. 90-113.10 or -113.11.

219. G.S. 90-96(a) and (a1) contain special provisions for sentencing first-time offenders who violate Article 5B.

Statute	Description of Offense	Punishment
Chapter 97: Workers' Compensation Act		
97-88.2(a)	False statement to obtain or deny benefit:	
	if amount is less than $1,000	Class 1 misdemeanor
	if amount is $1,000 or more	Class H felony[220]
97-88.2(c)	Threatening criminal prosecution to coerce employee to agree to or forego compensation	Class H felony[221]
Chapter 105: Taxation		
105-236(7)	Attempting to evade or defeat tax	Class H felony[222]
105-236(8)	Failing to collect, withhold, or pay over tax	Class 1 misdemeanor
105-236(9)	Failing to file return, supply information, or pay tax	Class 1 misdemeanor
105-236(9a)	Aiding presentation of false return	Class H felony[223]
Chapter 108A: Social Services		
108A-39(a)	Welfare fraud if value wrongfully received is $400 or less	Class 1 misdemeanor
108A-39(b)	Welfare fraud if value wrongfully received exceeds $400	Class I felony
108A-53(a)	Fraudulently obtaining or transferring food stamps:[224]	
	if value wrongfully received is $400 or less	Class 1 misdemeanor
	if value wrongfully received exceeds $400	Class I felony
108A-53(b)	Presenting fraudulently obtained food stamps	Class 1 misdemeanor
108A-53(c)	Receiving fraudulently obtained food stamps	Class 1 misdemeanor
108A-53.1(a)	Unlawful purchase, sale, or distribution of food stamps, or possession with intent to sell or distribute	Class H felony[225]

220. For offenses committed on or after Oct. 1, 1994, and before Oct. 1, 1997, this offense was a Class 1 misdemeanor.

221. *See* note 220.

222. For offenses committed on or after Oct. 1, 1994, and before Dec. 1, 1998, this offense was a Class I felony and could include a fine up to $25,000.

223. For offenses committed on or after Oct. 1, 1994, and before Dec. 1, 1998, this offense was a Class I felony and could include a fine up to $10,000.

224. For offenses committed on or after Dec. 1, 1995, and before Dec. 1, 1996, the dividing line between a felony and misdemeanor offense was $1,000. For offenses committed on or after Oct. 1, 1994, and before Dec. 1, 1995, the dividing line was $2,000.

225. G.S. 108A-53.1 applies to offenses committed on or after Dec. 1, 1997.

Statute	Description of Offense	Punishment
108A-53.1(b)	Unlawful use, transfer, acquisition, alteration, or possession of food stamps:[226]	
	if value is less than $100	Class 1 misdemeanor
	if value is $100 to $499	Class A1 misdemeanor
	if value is $500 to $999	Class I felony
	if value is $1000 or more	Class H felony
108A-63	Medicaid fraud by provider	Class I felony
108A-64	Medicaid fraud by recipient:[227]	
	if value wrongfully received is $400 or less	Class 1 misdemeanor
	if value wrongfully received exceeds $400	Class I felony

Chapter 113: Conservation and Development

Statute	Description of Offense	Punishment
113-60.21 to -60.29	Violating open-burning laws	Class 3 misdemeanor

Chapter 115C: Elementary and Secondary Education

Statute	Description of Offense	Punishment
115C-288(g)	Failure by principal to report offense committed on school grounds	Class 3 misdemeanor[228]
115C-378, -380	Failing to require child to attend school	Class 3 misdemeanor

Chapter 130A: Public Health

Statute	Description of Offense	Punishment
130A-25(a), 14-3(a)	Public health violation other than violation of health control measures	Class 1 misdemeanor[229]
130A-185, -25(a), 14-3(a)	Failure by owner to have dog or cat vaccinated against rabies	Class 1 misdemeanor

226. *See* note 225.

227. Effective for offenses committed on or after Dec. 1, 1995, G.S. 108A-64(b1) added the following offense: obtaining or attempting to obtain money, services, or any other thing of value to which the person is not entitled as a Medicaid recipient or otherwise deliberately misusing a Medicaid identification card.

228. This punishment became effective Nov. 1, 1997.

229. Violations of health control measures are not subject to structured sentencing. *See* G.S. 15A-1340.10 (exempting such violations from structured sentencing). Violating a health control measure is a misdemeanor, punishable by a term of imprisonment of no more than 2 years in McCain Hospital, the North Carolina Correctional Center for Women, or any other facility designated by the Secretary of Correction after consultation with the State Health Director. The person may not be released before completion of the prison term unless the court determines that release would not create a danger to the public health. *See* G.S. 130A-25(b), (c) (specifying punishment for violations of control measures and quarantines under G.S. 130A-144 and -145).

Statute	Description of Offense	Punishment
Chapter 136: Roads and Highways		
136-18(5)	Violating Department of Transportation rules	Class 1 misdemeanor
136-90	Obstructing highway	Class 1 misdemeanor
136-91	Placing injurious object in road	Class 3 misdemeanor
136-197	Boarding train by intoxicated person after being forbidden	Class 1 misdemeanor[230]
Chapter 148: State Prison System		
148-45(a)	Escape from state prison system by misdemeanant (first offense)	Class 1 misdemeanor[231]
148-45(b)	Escape from state prison system:	
	by felon	Class H felony[232]
	by any person previously convicted of escape or attempted escape from state prison system	Class H felony[233]
148-45(d)	Aiding escape from state prison system	Class 1 misdemeanor
148-46.1	Self injury by prisoner to avoid assigned work	Class H felony[234]

230. G.S. 136-197 applies to offenses committed on or after Sept. 4, 1998.

231. G.S. 148-45(g)(1) provides that failure to return to the custody of the Department of Correction from work release or other temporary release is treated as escape, punishable under the applicable sections of G.S. 148-45. *See* State v. Washington, 54 N.C. App. 683, 284 S.E.2d 330 (1981) (although failure to return from work release in violation of subsection (g) of G.S. 148-45 is punishable as escape under subsection (a) or (b), it is a separate offense and must be specifically charged). G.S. 148-45(g)(2) provides that if a person who would otherwise be guilty of a first violation of subsection (g)(1) (failure to return from temporary release) voluntarily returns within 24 hours, he or she shall not be charged with escape. If a person commits a subsequent violation of subsection (g)(1), however, failure to return is an escape even if the person returns within 24 hours. For offenses committed on or after Oct. 1, 1994, and before Dec. 1, 1997, escape was a Class I felony.

232. *See* note 231.

233. *See* note 231.

234. For offenses committed on or after Oct. 1, 1994, and before Dec. 1, 1997, this offense was a Class I felony.

Index to Punishment Chart for North Carolina Crimes

References in this index are to statute numbers, except that common-law offenses are listed by page number. Each statutory or page reference corresponds to a separate entry in Part 1, "Punishment Chart for North Carolina Crimes." For example, the statutory references for "assault on government official" are 14-33(c)(4) and 14-34.2; each statute number refers to a separate offense in the punishment chart. Some offenses in the punishment chart have multiple statutory references, but only the first statute number is listed in the index.

Part 2
Punishment Chart for North Carolina Motor Vehicle Offenses

Detailed Table of Contents

Description of Punishment Chart for Motor Vehicle Offenses

This chart lists (in numerical order by section number) the more common and/or more important motor vehicle offenses. The first column gives the section number that creates the offense, and an asterisk (*) beside the section number indicates that the court must require the defendant (if convicted) to surrender his or her driver's license pursuant to Chapter 20, Section 24(a), of the North Carolina General Statutes [hereinafter G.S.]; the clerk of court must then give the defendant a dated receipt. The second column briefly describes the offense; there is no attempt to cover all of the elements of a particular offense in this description. The third column gives the section number of the statute that contains the punishment, and the last column indicates whether the punishment is an infraction, misdemeanor, felony, etc.

Each year the chief district court judges adopt a "waiver list," designating those offenses that are waiverable and those where a mandatory court appearance is required; those requiring a mandatory court appearance are so indicated in the last column. All other offenses are waiverable—meaning that they can be paid off without going to court. (The 1999 waiver list is contained at Appendix A to this chart.)

Driver's license revocations and suspensions are indicated in the footnotes for many of the more serious offenses. The abbreviations DMV and CMV are used to refer to the Division of Motor Vehicles and the Commissioner of Motor Vehicles; DOT refers to the North Carolina Department of Transportation; app. stands for appearance. G.S. 20-16, "Authority of Division to suspend license," sets out the North Carolina driver's license point system. It can be found in its entirety in Appendix B.

Punishment Chart for North Carolina Motor Vehicle Offenses

Offense Statute	Description of Offense	Punishment Statute	Punishment
Driver's License Violations			
Driving without License or Violating Restrictions			
20-7(a)	Operating motor vehicle without N.C. license (see G.S. 20-8 for exceptions)	20-35	Class 2 misdemeanor
20-7 (a)	Driving class of motor vehicle which driver's license does not entitle a person to drive	20-35	Class 2 misdemeanor
20-7(a)	Failure to carry license while operating vehicle [production of license valid at time of charge is a good defense, G.S. 20-35(c)]	20-35	Class 2 misdemeanor
20-7 (al)	Operating motorcycle without having proper driver's license endorsement	2-35	Class 2 misdemeanor
20-7 (e)	Operating vehicle in violation of restriction noted on license	20-35	Class 2 misdemeanor
20-7(l),(m)	Operating vehicle in violation of restriction noted on instruction or learner's permit	20-35	Class 2 misdemeanor
Age Limits			
20-10	Operating a public passenger vehicle if under age 18	20-35	Class 2 misdemeanor
20-10	Operating any road machine, tractor, etc., on state highway, age 14 or under	20-35	Class 2 misdemeanor
20-10.1	Unlawful for any person under age 16 to drive a moped on highway or public vehicular area	20-35	Class 2 misdemeanor

Offense Statute	Description of Offense	Punishment Statute	Punishment
Learner's Permit			
20-11(c), (e), (h)	Unlawful for any person to drive in violation of restriction of limited learner's permit, limited provisional license, or temporary permit. Violation of time or supervising driver restriction is driving without license (NOL). Any other restriction violation is an infraction[1]	20-11(l) 20-35 20-176	Class 2 misdemeanor Infraction
Impaired Driving Instructor			
20-12.1	Unlawful to instruct while impaired[2, 3]	20-35	Class 2 misdemeanor (mandatory app.)
Driving with Suspended or Revoked License			
20-16.1(b)*	Violating limited driving privilege for excessive speeding[4]	20-16.1(b)(4) 20-28(a)	Class 1 misdemeanor (mandatory app.)
20-28(a)*	Driving while license is suspended or revoked[5]	20-28(a)	Class 1 misdemeanor (mandatory app.)
20-28(a)	Driving of vehicle by a restoree of a suspended or revoked license without the requisite financial responsibility	20-28(a) 20-7 20-35	Class 2 misdemeanor (mandatory app.)
20-28(al)	Driving without reclaiming license revoked pursuant to G.S. 20-16.5. (Immediate Civil Revocation)[6]	20-28(a1) 20-35	Class 2 misdemeanor
20-28(d)*	Driving a vehicle while person is disqualified and revoked[7]	20-28(d) 20-28(a), (b)	Class 1 misdemeanor (mandatory app.)

*Pursuant to G.S. 20-24(a), the court must require the driver convicted of this offense to surrender his or her driver's license to the court.

1. *See* G.S. 20-11(m) for insurance status of permittee.

2. G.S. 20-16(8a) authorizes DMV to suspend a license for "impaired instruction under 20-12.1," for a period of up to 1 year pursuant to G.S. 20-19(c).

3. This is an implied consent offense under G.S. 20-16.2.

4. Under G.S. 20-16.1(b)(4) the punishment is the same as for driving while license suspended in violation of G.S. 20-28.

5. For a first offense under this section, the license is revoked for an additional year; for a second offense, 2 additional years; a third or subsequent offense brings permanent revocation. The licensee is entitled to apply for restoration of the license early according to schedule set forth in G.S. 20-28(c).

6. A person convicted of driving while license revoked under these circumstances is treated as if convicted of driving without a license (NOL) for purposes of punishment and points (G.S. 20-28(a1)).

7. Driver is treated as if revoked under 20-28(a).

Offense Statute	Description of Offense	Punishment Statute	Punishment
20-28(d)	Driving a commercial motor vehicle during disqualification[8]	20-28(d)	Class 1 misdemeanor (mandatory app.)

Illegal Activity Relating to License

Offense Statute	Description of Offense	Punishment Statute	Punishment
20-29	Refusing to give uniformed officer information required by statute, such as name, address, or vehicle owner; or giving false information; or refusing to surrender or produce license upon demand of court or DMV	20-29	Class 2 misdemeanor
20-29	Driver of a car involved in an accident refusing to give information required by statute	20-29	Class 2 misdemeanor
20-29.1	Failure to observe restrictions imposed by DMV about the kinds of vehicles a licensee may operate	20-7 20-29.1 20-35	Class 2 misdemeanor
20-30(1)	Displaying or possessing any license or learner's permit known to be invalid[9]	20-35 20-16(a) (6) 20-19(c)	Class 2 misdemeanor (mandatory app.)
20-30(2)	Counterfeiting, selling, lending, or knowingly permitting the use of any driver's license or learner's permit by one not entitled thereto[9]	20-35 20-16(a) (6) 20-19(c)	Class 2 misdemeanor (mandatory app.)
20-30(3)	Displaying or representing as one's own a license not issued to the person displaying it[9]	20-35 20-16(a) (6) 20-19(c)	Class 2 misdemeanor (mandatory app.)
20-30(4)	Refusing to surrender to DMV a driver's license that has been revoked or suspended	20-35	Class 2 misdemeanor (mandatory app.)
20-30(5)*	Using or allowing others to use false names and addresses in license applications or renewals[10]	20-35 20-17(8) 20-19(f)	Class 2 misdemeanor (mandatory app.)
20-30(5)*	Making false statements, concealing material facts, or otherwise committing a fraud in applying for a license or permit[10]	20-35 20-17(8) 20-19(f)	Class 2 misdemeanor (mandatory app.)
20-30(6)	Reproducing or possessing a reproduced copy of a license or permit	20-35	Class 2 misdemeanor (mandatory app.)
20-30(7)	Offering simulated license for sale	20-30(7)	Class I felony (mandatory app.)
20-30(8)	To possess more than one commercial license, or to possess a commercial license and a regular license	20-35	Class 2 misdemeanor (mandatory app.)

*Pursuant to G.S. 20-24(a), the court must require the driver convicted of this offense to surrender his or her driver's license to the court.

8. G.S. 20-28(d) provides additional disqualification periods for this offense.

9. Under G.S. 20-16(a)(6) and -19(c), DMV may suspend a person's license for 1 year or less upon conviction of this offense.

10. Under G.S. 20-17(8) and -19(f), DMV must revoke a person's license for 1 year upon conviction of this offense.

Offense Statute	Description of Offense	Punishment Statute	Punishment
20-31*	Making a false affidavit or knowingly swearing or affirming falsely to any matter or thing required by the statutes to be sworn to[10]	20-31 20-17(5)	Class I felony (mandatory app.)
20-32	Causing or permitting an unlicensed minor to drive on a highway	20-35	Class 2 misdemeanor
20-34	Allowing motor vehicle to be driven in violation of license law	20-35	Class 2 misdemeanor (mandatory app.)

Parking Privileges for Handicapped Drivers

Offense Statute	Description of Offense	Punishment Statute	Punishment
20-37.6(c3)	Selling of a handicapped license plate or windshield placard	20-37.6(c3) 20-176(c)	Class 2 misdemeanor (mandatory app.)
20-37.6(e)(1)	Parking in a handicapped space without displaying a handicapped license tag or windshield placard[11]	20-37.6(f)(1)	Infraction
20-37.6(e)(2)	Using or attempting to use handicapped license tag or windshield placard when not entitled to do so[11]	20-37.6(f)(1)	Infraction
20-37.6(e)(3)	Parking in front of a handicapped ramp or curb cut[11]	20-37.6(f)(1)	Infraction
20-37.6(e)(4)	Those responsible for designating parking spaces as handicapped using signs not conforming to G.S. 30-37.6(d)[11]	20-37.6(f)(2)	Infraction

Special I.D. Card

Offense Statute	Description of Offense	Punishment Statute	Punishment
20-37.7	Engaging in fraud or misrepresentation in applying for and using a special identification card	20-37.7(e)	Class 2 misdemeanor (mandatory app.)

Commercial Licenses

Offense Statute	Description of Offense	Punishment Statute	Punishment
20-37.12 (a)	Driving a commercial vehicle without a valid commercial driver's license with applicable endorsements[12]	20-37.21 (a)	Class 3 misdemeanor (mandatory app.)
20-37.12(b)	Driving a commercial vehicle in violation of an out-of-service order[12]	20-37.21 (a), 20-17.4	Class 3 misdemeanor (mandatory app.)

*Pursuant to G.S. 20-24(a), the court must require the driver convicted of this offense to surrender his or her driver's license to the court.

10. Under G.S. 20-17(8) and -19(f), DMV must revoke a person's license for 1 year upon conviction of this offense.

11. Penalty of $50 to $100.

12. Fined no less than $250 for first offense and no less than $500 for second or subsequent offense. Driving commercial vehicle in violation of "out-of-service order" results in disqualification to drive commercial vehicle for 90 days to 3 years.

Offense Statute	Description of Offense	Punishment Statute	Punishment
20-37.18(a)	Possessing a commercial driver's license and failing to notify DMV within 30 days of a traffic conviction[13]	20-37.21(b)	Infraction
20-37.18(b)	Possessing a commercial driver's license and failing to notify the employer within 30 days of a traffic conviction[13]	20-37.21(b)	Infraction
20-37.18(c)	Failing to notify the employer on the next business day that the commercial driver's license has been suspended, revoked, or canceled or that the privilege to drive a commercial vehicle has been lost[13]	20-37.21(b)	Infraction
20-37.19(a)	Failure to require an employee to notify the employer that commercial driver's license has been suspended, revoked, or canceled or the privilege lost[14]	20-37.21(c)	Infraction
20-37.19(b)(1)	Knowingly allowing, permitting, or authorizing a driver to drive a commercial vehicle while the commercial license has been suspended, revoked, or canceled, etc.[14]	20-37.21(c)	Infraction
20-37.19(b)(2)	Knowingly allowing, permitting, or authorizing a driver to drive a commercial vehicle when the driver has more than one driver's license[14]	20-37.21(c)	Infraction

Vehicle Registration

Offense Statute	Description of Offense	Punishment Statute	Punishment
20-50	Owning a vehicle which is not registered with DMV or which is not displaying current registration plates (unless vehicle is exempt from registration by statute)	20-176(a), (c)	Class 2 misdemeanor
20-57(c)	Failure to display registration card	20-176(a), (c)	Class 2 misdemeanor
20-63(a)	Willfully failing to surrender illegible registration plates upon request of DMV	20-63(a)	Class 2 misdemeanor
20-63(d)	Failing to place registration plate at proper place on vehicle	20-176(a), (c)	Class 2 misdemeanor
20-63(e)	Failing to clean registration plates after being requested to do so by an officer	20-63(e)	Class 3 misdemeanor
20-63(f)	Willfully operating vehicle with a registration plate which has been altered	20-63(f)	Class 2 misdemeanor (mandatory app.)
20-63(g)	Willfully altering, disguising, or concealing numbers on a registration plate	20-63(g)	Class 2 misdemeanor (mandatory app.)
20-71(a)	Altering certificate of title, registration card, or application for such with fraudulent intent	20-71(a) 20-177	Class I felony (mandatory app.)

13. Penalty of no less than $100 and no more than $500.

14. Penalty of no less than $500 and no more than $1,000.

Offense Statute	Description of Offense	Punishment Statute	Punishment
20-71(a)	Forging or counterfeiting certificate of title or registration card	20-71 (a) 20-177	Class I felony (mandatory app.)
20-71(a)	Knowingly using an altered, forged, or falsified certificate of title or registration card	20-71(a) 20-177	Class I felony (mandatory app.)
20-71(b)	Possessing a blank N.C. certificate of title or facsimile with fraudulent intent	20-71(b)	Class I felony (mandatory app.)
Salvage Titles			
20-71.4(a)	Failing to disclose that a vehicle was flooded, reconstructed, or salvaged or that it was damaged when repair cost was over 25% of fair market value	20-71.4(a)	Class 2 misdemeanor
20-71.4(b)	Removing the title or supporting documents to any vehicle to conceal damage	20-71.4(b)	Class 2 misdemeanor
Transfer of Title or Interest			
20-72(b)	Delivering or accepting a certificate of title assigned in blank	20-72(b)	Class 2 misdemeanor (mandatory app.)
20-73(a)	Failing to apply for certificate of title within required time[15]	20-73(c)	Class 2 misdemeanor
20-74	Knowingly making a false statement about the date a vehicle was sold or acquired	20-74	Class 3 misdemeanor
Dealer Plates			
20-79(e)(1)	Driving a vehicle with dealer license plates in violation of restrictions[16]	20-79(e)(1)	Infraction
Car Theft and Related Offenses			
20-102.1	Knowingly making false report of vehicle theft to DMV or officer	20-102.1	Class 2 misdemeanor
20-106	Receiving or transferring stolen vehicles	20-106	Class H felony (mandatory app.)
20-106.1	Failure to return a rented vehicle with intent to defraud	20-106.1	Class I felony (mandatory app.)
20-107(a)	Willfully tampering with or removing parts from a vehicle without owner's consent	20-107(a)	Class 2 misdemeanor
20-107(b)	Tampering with or attempting to steal vehicle	20-107(b)	Class 2 misdemeanor

15. Subject to a civil penalty of $10.

16. Subject to a penalty of $50.

Offense Statute	Description of Offense	Punishment Statute	Punishment
20-108(a)	Knowingly possessing, selling, receiving, etc., a vehicle that has had any identification or serial number altered or removed	20-108(a)	Class 2 misdemeanor
20-109(a)	Knowingly altering or removing any serial or identification numbers on parts of a vehicle, or knowingly placing an unauthorized number on any vehicle or part or allowing such actions	20-109(a)	Class I felony (mandatory app.)
20-109(b)	Intentionally concealing or misrepresenting true identity of a vehicle by altering or defacing a serial number, or allowing such actions on one's vehicle, or using or selling parts of a vehicle containing serial numbers with intent to conceal the identity of the vehicle	20-109(b)	Class I felony (mandatory app.)

Violation of Registration Provisions

Offense Statute	Description of Offense	Punishment Statute	Punishment
20-111(1)	Operating a vehicle which is not registered with DMV or which is not displaying current registration plates	20-176(a), (c)	Class 2 misdemeanor
20-111(2)	Knowingly displaying or possessing an altered, expired, or revoked registration card or plate	20-176(a), (c)	Class 2 misdemeanor (mandatory app.)
20-111(3)	Giving, lending, or borrowing a registration plate for use on another vehicle	20-111(3)	Class 3 misdemeanor
20-111(4)	Failing to surrender to DMV, upon demand, any title certificate, registration card, or plate which has been suspended or canceled	20-176(a), (c)	Class 2 misdemeanor
20-111(5)	Using false names or addresses or concealing or misrepresenting material facts in registration applications	20-111(5)	Class 1 misdemeanor
20-111(6)	Giving, lending, selling, or obtaining any title certificate for any purpose other than registration, sale, etc., of vehicle for which issued	20-111(6)	Class 2 misdemeanor

Perjury

Offense Statute	Description of Offense	Punishment Statute	Punishment
20-112*	Knowingly making any false affidavit or swearing or affirming falsely	20-112 20-17(5)	Class I felony (mandatory app.)

Failure to Obey Directions of Police or Firefighters

Offense Statute	Description of Offense	Punishment Statute	Punishment
20-114.1(a)	Willfully failing or refusing to comply with lawful orders of law-enforcement officer related to control of traffic	20-176(a), (c)	Class 2 misdemeanor (mandatory app.)

*Pursuant to G.S. 20-24(a), the court must require the driver convicted of this offense to surrender his or her driver's license to the court.

Offense Statute	Description of Offense	Punishment Statute	Punishment
20-114.1(b)	Willfully failing or refusing to comply with lawful orders of firefighters (at scene of fire) or rescue squads (at scene of an accident) related to traffic control	20-176(a), (c)	Class 2 misdemeanor (mandatory app.)

Equipment Violations

Tires

20-122.1	Driving with unsafe tires	20-115 20-176(a), (b)	Infraction

Steering Mechanism

20-123.1	Failing to maintain steering mechanism in good working order	20-115 20-176(a), (b)	Infraction

Speedometer

20-123.2	Operating a vehicle without a working speedometer[17]	20-123.2(b)	Infraction

Brakes

20-124(a)	Absence of brakes sufficient to stop and control vehicle	20-115 20-176(a), (b)	Infraction
20-124(a)	Failure to maintain brakes in conformity with regulations	20-115 20-176(a), (b)	Infraction
20-124(c)	Failure to maintain originally equipped brakes, including failure to maintain two separate means of applying brakes	20-115 20-176(a), (b)	Infraction
20-124(d)	Absence of at least one brake on motorcycle used on highway	20-115 20-176(a), (b)	Infraction
20-124(e)	Absence on trucks of brakes sufficient to stop vehicle within required distances	20-115 20-176(a), (b)	Infraction
20-124(el)	Absence of brakes acting on all wheels on specified trucks or tractor-trucks with trailers	20-115 20-176(a), (b)	Infraction

Selling Unapproved Brake Fluid or Lining

20-124(h)	Selling any unapproved brake fluid or lining	20-124(h)	Class 2 misdemeanor

17. Penalty of no more than $25 and no license or insurance points.

Offense Statute	Description of Offense	Punishment Statute	Punishment
Horns and Warning Devices			
20-125(a)	Driving a vehicle without a horn audible up to 200 feet in normal conditions	20-115 20-176(a), (b)	Infraction
20-125(a)	Using a siren, compression, or spark plug whistle when not allowed	20-115 20-176(a), (b)	Infraction
20-125(a)	Using a horn for other than a reasonable warning or making any unnecessary loud or harsh sound by horn or other warning device	20-115 20-176(a), (b)	Infraction
Mirrors			
20-126(a)	Driving a vehicle on streets without a rearview mirror which provides unobstructed view (exempted vehicles in statute)	20-115 20-176(a), (b)	Infraction
20-126(a)	Driving a loaded vehicle which renders a rearview mirror ineffective without using a mirror that reflects the rear view	20-115 20-176(a), (b)	Infraction
20-126(b)	Operating a vehicle without an outside mirror on the driver's side (for vehicles assembled or sold after 1965)	20-115 20-176(a), (b)	Infraction
20-126(c)	Operating a motorcycle on streets without a rearview mirror that provides an unobstructed view of at least 200 feet	20-115 20-176(a), (b)	Infraction
Windshields			
20-127(a)	Operating a vehicle without a windshield wiper for cleaning snow, rain, moisture, etc., from the front windshield	20-115 20-176(a), (b)	Infraction
20-127(b)	Having tinted windows or windshield not meeting state standards	20-127(d) 20-176(a), (c)	Class 2 misdemeanor
Mufflers			
20-128(a)	Driving vehicle when muffler not in sufficiently good working order to prevent excessive noise or smoke	20-115 20-176(a), (b)	Infraction
20-128(b)	Using a muffler cut-out	20-115 20-176(a), (b)	Infraction
20-128(c)	Operating a motor vehicle without required emission control devices	20-115 20-176(a), (b)	Infraction
20-128.1(a)	Operating a gasoline-powered vehicle that emits visible air contaminants for longer than 5 seconds[18]	20-128.1(d) 20-176(a), (b)	Infraction

18. A person charged under this section has 30 days in which to repair the vehicle.

Offense Statute	Description of Offense	Punishment Statute	Punishment
20-128.1(a)	Operating a diesel-powered vehicle that emits visible contaminants of a specific shade or density for longer than 5 seconds[18]	20-128.1(d) 20-176 (a), (b)	Infraction

Lights

Offense Statute	Description of Offense	Punishment Statute	Punishment
20-129(a)(1)	Failing to have lights on from sunset to sunrise	20-115 20-176(a), (b)	Infraction
20-129(a)(2)	Failing to have lights on when a person cannot be seen clearly 400 feet ahead	20-115 20-176(a), (b)	Infraction
20-129(a)(4)	Failing to have lights on when windshield wipers are in use due to rain, fog, etc.[19]	20-129(a)(4)	Infraction
20-129(b)	Absence on vehicle of at least two headlamps (statute lists exceptions)	20-115 20-176(a), (b)	Infraction
20-129(c)	Absence on motorcycle of headlamp complying with requirements of statute	20-115 20-176(a), (b)	Infraction
20-129(c)	Failure to keep motorcycle lamps lighted while motorcycle in use on highway or public vehicular area	20-115 20-176(a), (b)	Infraction
20-129(d)	Absence of any of required rear lamps as listed in statute	20-115 20-176(a), (b)	Infraction
20-129(e)	Absence of required lamps or reflectors on bicycles used at night	20-115 20-176(a), (b)	Infraction
20-129(f)	Absence of required lights on other vehicles (farm tractors, etc.; see statute for details)	20-115 20-176(a), (b)	Infraction
20-129(g)	Selling or operating a vehicle or motorcycle without a stop lamp	20-115 20-176(a), (b)	Infraction
20-129.1(1)	Absence of two reflectors and one stop light on rear of bus or truck	20-115 20-176(a), (b)	Infraction
20-129.1(2)	Absence of additional specified lights and reflectors on certain trucks or buses	20-115 20-176(a), (b)	Infraction
20-129.1(3)	Absence of two clearance lamps on front, and one stop light at rear, on truck tractor	20-115 20-176(a), (b)	Infraction
20-129.1(4)	Absence of specified lights and reflectors on certain trailers or semi-trailers	20-115 20-176(a), (b)	Infraction
20-129.1(5)	Absence of specified lights and reflectors on certain large pole-trailers	20-115 20-176(a), (b)	Infraction
20-129.1(6)	Absence of required reflectors and stop lights on certain smaller trailers	20-115 20-176(a), (b)	Infraction
20-129.1(7),	Failure on vehicle of front-clearance lamps to reflect an amber color, or rear lamps and brake lights to reflect a red color	20-115 20-176(a), (b)	Infraction

18. A person charged under this section has 30 days in which to repair the vehicle.

19. Fined $5, but no court costs or license or insurance points.

Offense Statute	Description of Offense	Punishment Statute	Punishment
20-129.1(10)	Absence of combination marker lamp mounted on the bottom side rail at or near the center of each side of certain trailers showing amber color	20-115 20-176(a), (b)	Infraction
20-130.1(a)	Installing or using a red light on a vehicle (see 20-130.1 (b) for vehicle exceptions)	20-130.1(e)	Class 1 misdemeanor (mandatory app.)
20-130.1(c)	Installing or using a blue light on a vehicle (see 20-130.1(d) for vehicle exceptions)	20-130.1(e)	Class 1 misdemeanor (mandatory app.)
20-130.3	Driving a vehicle in forward motion while displaying white or clear lights on the rear of the vehicle (does not apply to backup lights)	20-115 20-176(a), (b)	Infraction
20-134	Failing at required times to display certain lights on the front and rear of a vehicle parked or stopped on a highway (attended or unattended)	20-115 20-176(a), (b)	Infraction

Seat Belts

Offense Statute	Description of Offense	Punishment Statute	Punishment
20-135.2A	Failure of driver or front seat occupant to have seat safety belt properly fastened[20]	20-135.2A(e)	Infraction
20-135.2B	Transporting children in the open bed of a pickup truck[20]	20-135.2B(c)	Infraction

Smoke Screens

Offense Statute	Description of Offense	Punishment Statute	Punishment
20-136*	Driving, using, or possessing a vehicle with a mechanism capable of discharging an unusual amount of smoke or gas, or possessing such device	20-136(b) 20-17(a)(3)	Class I felony (mandatory app.)

Child Restraint Systems

Offense Statute	Description of Offense	Punishment Statute	Punishment
20-137.1	Transporting child less than 12 years of age without having him or her secured in passenger restraint system (car safety seat) meeting federal standards. Requirement may be met when child is 4 years of age or older by securing him or her in a seat safety belt[21]	20-137.1(c)	Infraction

*Pursuant to G.S. 20-24(a), the court must require the driver convicted of this offense to surrender his or her driver's license to the court.

20. Fined $25; no court costs. Under G.S. 20-135.2A(f) and -135.2B(d), no license or insurance points are assessed.

21. Maximum $25 penalty, but no license or insurance points.

Offense Statute	Description of Offense	Punishment Statute	Punishment
Rules of the Road Violations			
Driving While Impaired			
20-138.1*	Driving a vehicle while impaired or after consuming sufficient alcohol so that, at any relevant time after driving, the driver has a concentration of .08[22]	20-138.1 (d) 20-179(g) 20-17(a)(2)	Level One: Up to $4,000 and 30 days to 24 months (mandatory app.)
20-138.1*	Driving a vehicle while impaired or after consuming sufficient alcohol so that, at any relevant time after driving, the driver has a concentration of .08[22]	20-138.1 (d) 20-179(h) 20-17(a)(2)	Level Two: Up to $2,000 and 7 days (minimum) to 12 months (mandatory app.)
20-138.1*	Driving a vehicle while impaired or after consuming sufficient alcohol so that, at any relevant time after driving, the driver has a concentration of .08[22]	20-138.1(d) 20-179(i) 20-17(a)(2)	Level Three: Up to $1,000 and 72 hours (minimum) to 6 months (mandatory app.)

*Pursuant to G.S. 20-24(a), the court must require the driver convicted of this offense to surrender his or her driver's license to the court.

22. The driving-while-impaired sentencing statute (G.S. 20-179) contains several unique provisions. The punishments listed in this chart are the minimums and maximums allowable under the statute for each level of punishment, but for each level there are other relevant sentencing provisions.

Level One: 30 days to 24 months in jail. At least 30 days must be imposed, and this sentence cannot be suspended unless the defendant serves at least 30 days in jail. There is also a fine of up to $4,000.

Level Two: 7 days to 12 months in jail. At least 7 days must be imposed, and this sentence cannot be suspended unless the defendant serves at least 7 days in jail as a condition of special probation. There is also a fine of up to $2,000.

Level Three: 72 hours to 6 months in jail. A minimum of 72 hours must be imposed, and this sentence can be suspended only if the defendant meets certain conditions. The judge must require that the defendant do at least one of three things: 1) not drive for at least 90 days; 2) perform at least 72 hours of community service; or 3) serve at least 72 hours in jail under the special probation statute. There is also a fine of up to $1,000.

Level Four: 48 hours to 120 days in jail. A minimum of 48 hours must be imposed, and this sentence can be suspended only if the defendant meets certain conditions. The judge must require that the defendant do at least one of three things: 1) not drive for 60 days; 2) perform 48 hours of community service; or 3) serve 48 hours in jail under the special probation statute. There is also a fine of up to $500.

Level Five: 24 hours to 60 days in jail. A minimum of 24 hours must be imposed, and this sentence can be suspended only if the defendant meets certain conditions. The judge must require that the defendant do at least one of three things: 1) not drive for 30 days; 2) perform 24 hours of community service; or 3) serve 24 hours in jail under the special probation statute. There is also a fine of up to $200.

Under any level of punishment, if the defendant is placed on probation a substance abuse assessment is required, as is education or treatment as required by G.S. 20-17.6.

Under G.S. 20-17(a)(2), DMV must revoke a driver's license when it receives a record of the driver's final conviction of "impaired driving under G.S. 20-138.1."

A trial judge (under G.S. 20-179.3) may allow a limited driving privilege if punishment level 3, 4, or 5 was imposed and the criteria established by that statute are met.

Offense Statute	Description of Offense	Punishment Statute	Punishment
20-138.1*	Driving a vehicle while impaired or after consuming sufficient alcohol so that, at any relevant time after driving, the driver has a concentration of .08[22]	20-138.1(d) 20-179(j) 20-17(a)(2)	Level Four: Up to $500 and 48 hours (minimum) to 120 days (mandatory app.)
20-138.1*	Driving a vehicle while impaired or after consuming sufficient alcohol so that, at any relevant time after driving, the driver has a concentration of .08[22]	20-138.1(d) 20-179(k) 20-17(a)(2)	Level Five: Up to $200 and 24 hours (minimum) to 60 days
20-138.2(a)*	Impaired driving in a commercial vehicle or after consuming sufficient alcohol so that, at any relevant time after driving, the driver has a concentration of .04[23]	20-138.2(e) 20-17(a)(2)	Class 1 misdemeanor (mandatory app.)
20-138.2A	Operating commercial vehicle after consuming alcohol[23]	20-138.2A(c) 20-179 20-17(a)(13) 20-17.4	Class 3 misdemeanor $100 penalty for first offense (mandatory app.)
20-138.2B*	Driving school bus, school activity bus or child care vehicle after consuming alcohol	20-138.2B(c) 20-17(a)(14) 20-179	Class 3 misdemeanor $100 penalty for first offense (mandatory app.)
20-138.3(a)*	Driving by person under age 21 after consuming alcohol or drugs[24]	20-138.3 (c) 20-13.2	Class 2 misdemeanor (mandatory app.)
20-138.5(a)*	Driving while impaired after being convicted of three or more offenses involving impaired driving within 7 years	20-138.5(b) 20-138.5(d)	Class F felony (mandatory app.)
20-138.7*	Transporting open container of alcoholic beverage after consuming alcohol[24]	20-138.7(e)	Class 3 misdemeanor for first offense (mandatory app.)

*Pursuant to G.S. 20-24(a), the court must require the driver convicted of this offense to surrender his or her driver's license to the court.

23. Under G.S. 20-17.4 a person convicted of this offense will be disqualified from driving a commercial vehicle. *See also* G.S. 20-17(a)(2)(b) for revocation provisions. (See G.S. 20-17(a)(13) and -17.4 for revocation and disqualification for driving commercial vehicle after consuming alcohol.)

24. G.S. 20-13.2 requires revocation of the driver's license for a violation of G.S. 20-138.3. G.S. 20-17(a)(12) requires revocation for a second conviction under G.S. 20-138.7.

Offense Statute	Description of Offense	Punishment Statute	Punishment
Reckless Driving[25]			
20-140(a)	Driving carelessly and heedlessly[25]	20-140(d)	Class 2 misdemeanor (mandatory app.)
20-140(b)	Driving without due caution[25]	20-140(d)	Class 2 misdemeanor (mandatory app.)
Use of Controlled-access Highways[26]			
20-140.3(1)	Driving across a curb, dividing section, or dividing line on controlled-access highways	20-176(a), (b)	Infraction
20-140.3(2)	Making a left, semicircular, or U-turn when there is no opening provided for that purpose in the dividing curb, separation, or line on controlled-access highways	20-176(a), (b)	Infraction
20-140.3(3)	Driving in the wrong lane or wrong direction on controlled-access highways	20-176(a), (b)	Infraction
20-140.3(4)	Driving onto or from any controlled-access highway when such entrances and exits are not established by public authority	20-176(a), (b)	Infraction
20-140.3(5)	Stopping, parking, or leaving a vehicle (attended or unattended) on any part of the right-of-way	20-176(a), (b)	Infraction
20-140.3(6)	Failing to yield the right-of-way when entering the highway to a vehicle already traveling on highway	20-176(a), (b)	Infraction
Motorcycles and Mopeds			
20-140.4(a)(1)	Operating a motorcycle or moped with more persons than it is designated to carry[27]	20-140.4(c) 20-135.2A(e), (f)	Infraction
20-140.4(a)(2)	Operating a motorcycle or moped without an approved safety helmet[27]	20-140.4(c) 20-135.2A(e), (f)	Infraction

25. Reckless driving violations are subject to the following provisions for revocation or suspension of license: discretionary suspension under G.S. 20-16(a)(9) and -19(a) is not to exceed 6 months for conviction of one or more charges of reckless driving (and *one* or more charges of speeding in excess of 55 mph and not more than 80 mph) within a 12-month period. Mandatory revocation under G.S. 20-17(a)(6), (7), and -19(f) is for 1 year for conviction upon one charge of reckless driving while illegally transporting intoxicants for the purpose of sale or for *two* charges of reckless driving in 12 months.

26. G.S. 136-89.58 also creates certain controlled-access road offenses that roughly parallel those in G.S. 20-140.3 (but are Class 2 misdemeanors).

27. Fined according to G.S. 20-135.2A(e) and (f), which calls for $25 and no court costs or license or insurance points.

Offense Statute	Description of Offense	Punishment Statute	Punishment
Speeding[28]			
20-141(a)	Driving faster than is reasonable and prudent under conditions	20-176(a), (b)	Infraction
20-141(b)	Operating vehicle in excess of following speeds (except where otherwise permitted in G.S. Ch. 20); 35 mph inside municipal corporate limits (for all vehicles); 55 mph outside municipal corporate limits (except as otherwise posted)	20-176(a), (b)	Infraction
20-141(e)	Violating speed limit set by local authority for streets *not* in state highway system (not to be more than 55 mph, and effective only if signs are posted)	20-176(a), (b)	Infraction
20-141(e1)	Violating speed limit on school property	20-141(e1)	Infraction (minimum $25)
20-141(f)	Violating speed limit set by local authority on streets in the state system and within corporate limits (effective when Department of Transportation passes concurring ordinance and signs are posted)	20-176(a), (b)	Infraction
20-141(g)	Violating minimum speed limit established on state highways or by local authorities (effective when appropriate signs giving notice are erected)	20-176(a), (b)	Infraction
20-141(j1)*	Driving more than 15 mph over speed limit[29]	20-141(j1) 20-16.1	Class 2 misdemeanor (mandatory app. if driver going over 55 mph)
20-141(j1)*	Driving over 80 mph[29]	20-141(j1) 20-16.1	Class 2 misdemeanor (mandatory app.)

*Pursuant to G.S. 20-24(a), the court must require the driver convicted of this offense to surrender his or her driver's license to the court.

28. All speeding violations are subject to the following provisions for suspension or revocation of license: discretionary suspension under G.S. 20-16(a)(10) and -19(b) is not to exceed 12 months if the person has been convicted of operating a motor vehicle over 75 mph where the maximum speed is less than 70 mph. Discretionary suspension under G.S. 20-16(a)(9) and -19(a) is not to exceed 6 months if the person has within a 12-month period been convicted of two or more charges of speeding over 55 mph and not more than 80 mph (or one or more charges of reckless driving and one or more charges of speeding in excess of 55 mph and not more than 80 mph). Mandatory suspension under G.S. 20-16.1 is for 30 days upon conviction of exceeding the speed limit by more than 15 mph if the person was also exceeding 55 mph at the time of the offense (or for 60 days upon conviction of a second or subsequent offense that occurred within 1 year of the first or prior offense). Same provisions apply if driver was exceeding 80 mph. A judge may grant limited driving privileges to a first offender under G.S. 20-16.1(a).

29. License suspended when speed is also over 55 mph. *See* G.S. 20-16.1. Mandatory app. required for more than 15 mph over limit while also over 55 mph.

Offense Statute	Description of Offense	Punishment Statute	Punishment
20-141(j2)	Driving in highway work zone in excess of posted speed[30]	20-141(j2)	Infraction (penalty of $100 to $250)
20-141(m)	Failing to reduce speed as necessary to avoid accident	20-176(a), (b)	Infraction

School Zones

Offense Statute	Description of Offense	Punishment Statute	Punishment
20-141.1	Violating speed limits set by the Board of Transportation or local authority for areas near schools (effective when signs are erected giving notice of school zone, speed limit, and days and hours)	20-176(a), (b)	Infraction (minimum penalty is $25)

Racing, Death by Vehicle, and Eluding Arrest

Offense Statute	Description of Offense	Punishment Statute	Punishment
20-141.3(a)*	Engaging in prearranged speed competition with another motor vehicle[31, 32]	20-141.3(a) 20-141.3(d)	Class 1 misdemeanor (mandatory app.)
20-141.3(b)	Willfully engaging in speed competition with another motor vehicle (not prearranged)[33]	20-141.3(b) 20-141.3(e)	Class 2 misdemeanor (mandatory app.)
20-141.3(c)*	Allowing or authorizing others to use one's motor vehicle in prearranged speed competition[31]	20-141.3(c) 20-141.3(d)	Class 1 misdemeanor (mandatory app.)
20-141.3(c)*	Placing or receiving a bet or wager on a prearranged speed competition[31]	20-141.3(c) 20-141.3(d)	Class 1 misdemeanor (mandatory app.)
20-141.4(al)*	Unintentionally causing death when driving while impaired[34]	20-141.4(b) 20-17(a)(9)	Class G felony (mandatory app.)
20-141.4(a2)*	Unintentionally causing death while engaged in violation other than DWI[34]	20-141.4(b) 20-17(a)(9)	Class 1 misdemeanor (mandatory app.)

*Pursuant to G.S. 20-24(a), the court must require the driver convicted of this offense to surrender his or her driver's license to the court.

30. Must pay $100 to $250 penalty.

31. Under G.S. 20-141.3(d) a driver convicted under this subsection has his or her license revoked for 3 years by the CMV; after 18 months DMV may issue a new license upon such terms and condition as it sees fit. G.S. 20-141.3(f) apparently makes the provisions of G.S. 20-24 applicable to this offense. Thus under G.S. 20-24(a), the court should pick up the defendant's driver's license.

32. Under G.S. 20-141.3(g) any vehicle used by a person convicted under this subsection is to be forfeited and sold at public auction. If the owner of the vehicle can show that it was used in prearranged racing without his or her consent and that there were no reasonable grounds to believe it would be so used, the vehicle may be recovered.

33. Under G.S. 20-141.3(e) the CMV may suspend for up to 1 year the license of a driver convicted under this subsection.

34. Under G.S. 20-17(a)(9) and -19(f), DMV must revoke for 1 year the license of a driver convicted of death by vehicle. If the offense involved impaired driving, then the revocation is permanent (G.S. 20-19(i)).

Offense Statute	Description of Offense	Punishment Statute	Punishment
20-141.5*	Speeding or otherwise attempting to elude arrest[35]	20-145.5	Class 1 misdemeanor or Class H felony (mandatory app.)

Failing to Stop for Railroad Signal or Tracks

Offense Statute	Description of Offense	Punishment Statute	Punishment
20-142.1(a)	Failing to stop at railroad grade crossing for electrical signal, gate, audible signal, or train in hazardous proximity to crossing	20-142.1 (d) 20-176(a), (b)	Infraction
20-142.1(b)	Driving through crossing gate while gate is closed, opening, or closing	20-142.1(d) 20-176(a), (b)	Infraction
20-142.2	Failure to stop at stop sign erected at dangerous railroad crossing by Department of Transportation	20-142.2 20-176(a), (b)	Infraction
20-142.3	Failing to stop; certain kinds of vehicles at all railroad crossings (exceptions noted in statute)	20-142.3(c) 20-176(a), (b)	Infraction
20-142.4(a),(b)	Crossing a railroad track with a tractor or with other equipment that normally has an operating speed of 5 mph or less without giving notice to a railroad superintendent	20-142.4(f) 20-176(a), (b)	Infraction
20-142.4(a),(c)	Crossing a railroad track with a tractor or with other equipment that normally has an operating speed of 5 mph or less without stopping first, listening and looking in both directions, and crossing when safe (doesn't apply to crossings where authorities have determined no trains are running)	20-142.4(f) 20-176(a), (b)	Infraction
20-142.4(a),(d)	Crossing a railroad track with a tractor or with other equipment that normally has an operating speed of 5 mph or less when signal, gates, or flagman are giving a warning	20-142.4(f) 20-176(a), (b)	Infraction
20-142.5	Driving into intersection, crosswalk, or railroad grade crossing in manner to obstruct vehicles, pedestrians, or trains	20-142.5 20-176(a), (b)	Infraction

Driving on Wrong Side of Road

Offense Statute	Description of Offense	Punishment Statute	Punishment
20-146(a)	Failing to drive on right half of highway of sufficient width (exceptions noted in statute)	20-176(a), (b)	Infraction
20-146(b)	Failing to drive in the right lane when driving below speed limit (except when passing or turning left)	20-176(a), (b)	Infraction
20-146(c)	Driving to left of center on a road with four or more lanes with two-way movement of traffic, except when authorized by signs or to avoid obstructions	20-176(a), (b)	Infraction

*Pursuant to G.S. 20-24(a), the court must require the driver convicted of this offense to surrender his or her driver's license to the court.

35. This offense is usually a misdemeanor, but it is a felony if any two of the aggravating factors in subsection (b) are present.

Offense Statute	Description of Offense	Punishment Statute	Punishment
20-146(d)(1)	Failure to: (a) drive within a single lane or (b) ascertain that a lane change can be made safely in a road with two lanes moving in same direction	20-176(a), (b)	Infraction
20-146(d)(2)	Driving in center lane of road with three or more lanes and two-way traffic, unless passing a vehicle, turning left, or in accordance with traffic signs	20-176(a), (b)	Infraction
20-146(d)(3)	Failure to: (a) obey traffic control devices directing that specified traffic use a designated lane or (b) obey traffic control devices designating lanes for traffic moving in certain direction	20-176(a), (b)	Infraction
20-146(d)(4)	Failure to obey signals as to lane changes	20-176(a)(b)	Infraction
20-146(e)	Impeding traffic by using lane next to median of dual-lane highway, unless traveling at speed limit or preparing to turn left (road must be posted)	20-176(a), (b)	Infraction
20-146.1(a)	Depriving a motorcycle of full use of a lane (except when two motorcyles are abreast in a single lane)	20-176(a), (b)	Infraction
20-146.1(b)	Operating more than two motorcycles abreast in single lane	20-176(a), (b)	Infraction
20-147	Failing to drive vehicle on right half of highway in crossing an intersection of two highways or of a highway and railroad right-of-way, unless the right side is obstructed	20-176(a), (b)	Infraction
20-148	Failing to pass a vehicle going in the opposite direction to the right, and leaving at least half of the road, if possible, for vehicle going in opposite direction	20-176(a), (b)	Infraction

Improper Passing

Offense Statute	Description of Offense	Punishment Statute	Punishment
20-149(a)	Passing another vehicle going in same direction without passing at least 2 feet to left of other vehicle (G.S. 20-150.1 permits passing on right in certain instances)	20-176(a), (b)	Infraction
20-149(a)	When passing on the left, returning to right lane before being safely clear of the passed vehicle	20-176(a), (b)	Infraction
20-149(b)	When being passed by another vehicle on the left, failing to give way to the right on hearing an audible warning signal from passing vehicle (not applicable if being passed on right under G.S. 20-150.1)[36]	20-176(a), (b) 20-149(b)(1) 20-149(b)(2)	Infraction; or Class 1 misdemeanor; or Class 2 misdemeanor (mandatory app.)

36. This offense is usually an infraction, but it is a misdemeanor if a collision results (Class 1 in case of serious injury, and Class 2 when there is any personal injury or property damage).

Offense Statute	Description of Offense	Punishment Statute	Punishment
20-150(a)	Passing on left when the left side of roadway is not clearly visible and free of traffic for sufficient distance to allow movement in safety	20-176(a), (b)	Infraction
20-150(b)	Passing on the crest of a grade or on a curve when driver cannot see roadway ahead for at least 500 feet	20-176(a), (b)	Infraction
20-150(c)	Passing at a railway grade crossing or at an intersection, unless allowed to do so by a police officer	20-176(a), (b)	Infraction
20-150(d)	Driving to left of a visible center line on the crest of a hill or on a curve	20-176(a), (b)	Infraction
20-150(e)	Passing another vehicle when signs or markings clearly indicate that passing should not be attempted	20-176(a), (b)	Infraction
20-150.1	Passing on right permitted	No violation	

Following Too Closely

Offense Statute	Description of Offense	Punishment Statute	Punishment
20-152(a)	Following a vehicle more closely than is reasonable and prudent, with regard for speed of other vehicles, traffic, and road conditions	20-176(a), (b)	Infraction
20-152(b)	When following a vehicle and being passed by another, failing to allow passing vehicle enough space to reenter his original lane of traffic (subject to exceptions listed in statute)	20-176(a), (b)	Infraction

Improper Turning

Offense Statute	Description of Offense	Punishment Statute	Punishment
20-153(a)	When approaching or turning right at an intersection, failing to keep vehicle as close as practicable to the right curb	20-176(a), (b)	Infraction
20-153(b)	When approaching intersection to turn left, failing to use extreme left-hand lane lawfully available	20-176(a), (b)	Infraction
20-153(b)	When turning left, failing to turn into a lane lawfully available to traffic leaving the intersection	20-176(a), (b)	Infraction
20-153(c)	Failure to obey lawful traffic control devices modifying the general turning rules of G.S. 20-153	20-176(a), (b)	Infraction
20-154(a)	Starting, stopping, or turning without first seeing that the movement can be made safely	20-176(a), (b)	Infraction
20-154(a)	Failure to sound the horn before making a movement that may affect pedestrians	20-176(a), (b)	Infraction
20-154(a)	Failure to give a signal of intention when stopping, starting, or turning when another vehicle may be affected (requirements for signals set out in statute)	20-176(a), (b)	Infraction
20-154(a)	Backing a vehicle in unsafe manner or in a manner that interferes with other traffic	20-176(a), (b)	Infraction

Offense Statute	Description of Offense	Punishment Statute	Punishment
Failing to Yield Right-of-way			
20-155(a)	When two vehicles enter intersection at approximately the same time, failure by driver on left to yield right-of-way	20-176(a), (b)	Infraction
20-155(b)	Failure to yield to oncoming traffic when turning left	20-176(a), (b)	Infraction
20-155(c)	Failure to yield to pedestrian at clearly marked crosswalks or regular pedestrian crossing (exceptions noted in statute)	20-176(a), (b)	Infraction
20-155(d)	When approaching a traffic circle, failing to yield to vehicle already in circle	20-176(a), (b)	Infraction
20-156(a)	When entering a public highway from a private road, failing to yield to traffic on the highway	20-176(a), (b)	Infraction
20-156(b)	Failure to yield right-of-way to police, fire, and other emergency vehicles with sirens and lights on	20-176(a), (b)	Infraction
20-157(a)	Upon approach of a fire, police, rescue vehicle, etc., with lights and siren on, failing to stop on right side of road until emergency vehicle passes	20-157(a)	Class 2 misdemeanor (mandatory app.)
Actions Prohibited in Emergencies			
20-157(b)	Following closer than one block any fire apparatus traveling in response to a fire alarm	20-176(a), (b)	Infraction
20-157(b)	Driving into or parking within one block where fire apparatus has stopped to answer an alarm	20-176(a), (b)	Infraction
20-157(c)	Outside of a city, following closer than 400 feet any fire apparatus traveling in response to a fire alarm	20-176(a), (b)	Infraction
20-157(c)	Outside of a city, driving into or parking within 400 feet of where fire apparatus has stopped to answer an alarm	20-176(a), (b)	Infraction
20-157(d)	Driving over a fire hose or any other equipment that is being used at a fire	20-176(a), (b)	Infraction
20-157(d)	Blocking firefighting apparatus from its source of supply	20-176(a), (b)	Infraction
20-157(e)	Parking or leaving a vehicle within 100 feet of police, fire, or rescue vehicles which are investigating or assisting at an accident	20-176(a), (b)	Infraction
Failing to Stop			
20-158(b)(1)	Failure to stop at intersections in obedience to posted stop sign or failure to yield right-of-way after stopping at stop sign	20-176(a), (b)	Infraction

Offense Statute	Description of Offense	Punishment Statute	Punishment
20-158(b)(2)	Failure to stop at intersection and yield right-of-way when traffic light emits a steady (or strobe) red light (also failure to enter intersection with due care when light is green)	20-176(a), (b)	Infraction
20-158(b)(3)	Failure to stop at intersection and yield when a flashing red light controls traffic in driver's lane	20-176(a), (b)	Infraction
20-158(b)(4)	Failure to proceed with caution and yield the right-of-way to vehicles in or approaching the intersection when a flashing yellow light controls the intersection	20-176(a), (b)	Infraction
20-158(b)(5)	When required to stop, (1) failing to stop at the appropriate marked line, (2) if no line, failing to stop before marked crosswalk, or (3) if no crosswalk, failing to stop at the point nearest the intersecting street where the driver has a view of approaching traffic	20-176(a), (b)	Infraction
20-158(c)(1)	Failure to obey a stop sign and yield right-of-way at place other than at an intersection	20-176(a), (b)	Infraction
20-158(c)(2)	Failure to obey a traffic light emitting a steady red light at place other than an intersection	20-176(a), (b)	Infraction
20-158(c)(3)	Failure to stop and yield to pedestrians or other vehicles at a flashing red light at place other than an intersection	20-176(a), (b)	Infraction
20-158(c)(4)	Failure to proceed with caution or yield at a yellow traffic light at place other than an intersection	20-176(a), (b)	Infraction
20-158(c)(5)	When required to stop, (1) failing to stop at the appropriate marked line, (2) if no line, failing to stop before marked crosswalk, or (3) if no crosswalk, failing to stop before proceeding past the signal device	20-176(a), (b)	Infraction

Failure to Yield at Yield Signs

20-158.1	Failure to yield at intersections where yield signs have been erected	20-176(a), (b)	Infraction

Driving through Safety Zones or on Sidewalks

20-160	Driving through or over a safety zone or driving on a sidewalk (except upon a driveway)	20-176(a), (b)	Infraction

Parking on Highway

20-161(a)	Outside of the city limits, parking or leaving a vehicle (attended or unattended) on the paved or main-traveled portion of road or bridge (unless vehicle is so disabled that it was impossible to avoid stopping)	20-176(a), (b)	Infraction

Offense Statute	Description of Offense	Punishment Statute	Punishment
20-161(b)	Outside of the city limits, parking or leaving a vehicle on the shoulder of the road (unless the vehicle can be clearly seen 200 feet away and does not obstruct normal traffic)	20-176(a), (b)	Infraction
20-161(c)	Failing to display warning signals on any truck, truck tractor, trailer, or semi-trailer in a manner required by the U.S. Department of Transportation and DMV as long as the vehicle is disabled on any portion of the highway	20-176(a), (b)	Infraction
20-161.1	Parking or leaving a vehicle at night on a road or on a side road entering a highway while shining its bright lights when facing oncoming traffic	20-176(a), (b)	Infraction
20-162(a)	Parking or leaving a vehicle (attended or unattended) (1) in front of a private driveway, (2) within 15 feet of a fire hydrant, (3) within 15 feet of fire station entrance, or (4) within 25 feet from the intersection of curb lines or, if none, then within 15 feet of the intersection of property lines	20-176(a), (b)	Infraction
20-162(b)	Parking or leaving a vehicle (attended or unattended) in a public vehicular area, street, highway, or road designated as a fire lane	20-176(a), (b)	Infraction
20-163	Leaving a vehicle unattended on a highway or public vehicular area without stopping engine, setting the brake, properly parking the vehicle	20-176(a), (b)	Infraction

Traveling Wrong Way on One-way Street

Offense Statute	Description of Offense	Punishment Statute	Punishment
20-165.1	Willfully going wrong way on one-way street designated and marked as such	20-176(a), (b)	Infraction

Accident Responsibility Laws

Offense Statute	Description of Offense	Punishment Statute	Punishment
20-166(a)*	Failure to stop by driver who knew or should have known he or she was involved in accident and that accident caused death or injury to any person[37]	20-166(a) 20-17(a)(4)	Class H felony (mandatory app.)
20-166(b)*	Failure of driver, as set forth in G.S. 20-166(a), to give required information and render assistance[37]	20-166(b) 20-17(a)(4)	Class 1 misdemeanor (mandatory app.)
20-166(c)	Failure of driver involved in accident causing property damage or personal injury or death (if driver did not know of injury or death) to stop at scene of accident	20-166(c)	Class 1 misdemeanor (mandatory app.)

*Pursuant to G.S. 20-24(a), the court must require the driver convicted of this offense to surrender his or her driver's license to the court.

37. G.S. 20-17(a)(4) and -19(f) require license revocation for 1 year.

Offense Statute	Description of Offense	Punishment Statute	Punishment
20-166(c1)	Failure of driver, as set forth in G.S. 20-166(c), to give required information	20-166(cl)	Class 1 misdemeanor (mandatory app.)
20-166.1(a)	Failure by driver to make required reports, by quickest means, to police if accident involves personal injury, death, or $1,000 or more in property damage	20-166.1(k) 20-176(c) 20-4.01(33b)	Class 2 misdemeanor (mandatory app.)
20-166.1(b)	Failure by driver involved in accident to make report of financial responsibility to DMV if so requested by DMV	20-166.1(k) 20-176(c)	Class 2 misdemeanor (mandatory app.)
20-166.1(c)	Failure by driver in collision with parked vehicle to make a timely report to owner and DMV	20-166.1(k) 20-176(c)	Class 2 misdemeanor (mandatory app.)
Transportation of Spent Nuclear Fuel			
20-167.1	Transporting spent nuclear fuel without notifying State Highway Patrol[38]	20-167.1(d)	Class 3 misdemeanor (mandatory app.)
Violations at Pedestrian Crosswalks			
20-173(a)	Where traffic control signals are not in operation, failing to yield to pedestrians at a marked crosswalk or at an unmarked crosswalk near an intersection	20-176(a), (b)	Infraction
20-173(b)	Passing a vehicle stopped at a pedestrian crosswalk	20-176(a), (b)	Infraction
20-173(c)	When entering highway from private road or driveway, failing to yield to pedestrians or bicyclists on sidewalk	20-176(a), (b3)	Infraction
Standing, Sitting, or Lying in Street			
20-174.1	Willfully standing, sitting, or lying on a highway in such a manner as to impede traffic	20-174.1(b)	Class 2 misdemeanor
Soliciting Rides, Employment, or Business on Highways			
20-175(a)	Standing in any portion of a state highway for purpose of soliciting a ride from a driver (except upon the shoulders of the highway)	20-176(a), (b)	Infraction
20-175(b)	Standing or loitering in the main traveled portion, including the shoulders and median, of a state highway or street, or stopping a vehicle for the purpose of soliciting employment, business, or contributions that impedes the movement of traffic	20-176(a), (b)	Infraction

38. Minimum fine is $500.

Offense Statute	Description of Offense	Punishment Statute	Punishment
Violating Limited Driving Privileges			
20-179.3(j)* 20-16.1(b)(4)	Violating conditions of limited driving privilege[39, 40]	20-179.3(j) 20-28(a)	Class 1 misdemeanor (mandatory app.)
Failure to Dim Lights			
20-181	Failure to dim headlights when meeting another vehicle or when following another at a distance of less than 200 feet	20-181	Infraction (up to $10 penalty)
Equipment Inspection Laws			
20-183.8(a)	Failing to display a current and valid inspection certificate[41]	20-183.8(a)	Infraction
20-183.8(c)	Forging inspection certificate	20-183.8(c)	Class I felony (mandatory app.)
Passing Stopped School Bus			
20-217(a)	Failure to stop and remain stopped when approaching a stopped school bus engaged in receiving or discharging passengers and while bus has mechanical stop signal (or stop lights) displayed (exceptions listed in statute)	20-217(e)	Class 2 misdemeanor (mandatory app.)
Bus Driver Rules			
20-217(d)	Stopping school bus to receive or discharge passengers where passengers would have to cross a roadway	20-217(e)	Class 2 misdemeanor
20-218(b)	Driving a loaded school bus over 45 mph, or driving a school activity bus over 55 mph	20-218(c)	Class 3 misdemeanor
20-218.2	Driving an activity bus for nonprofit organization for a nonprofit purpose over 55 mph	20-218.2	Class 3 misdemeanor

*Pursuant to G.S. 20-24(a), the court must require the driver convicted of this offense to surrender his or her driver's license to the court.

39. Under G.S. 20-16.1(b)(4) the punishment is the same as for driving while license suspended in violation of G.S. 20-28.

40. For a first offense under this section, the license is revoked for an additional year; for a second offense, 2 additional years; a third or subsequent offense brings permanent revocation. The licensee is entitled to apply for restoration of the license early according to schedule set forth in G.S. 20-28(c).

41. Penalty of no more than $50.

Offense Statute	Description of Offense	Punishment Statute	Punishment
Insurance Violations			
20-313(a)	Operating or allowing one's vehicle registered in this state to be operated without the "required financial responsibility"	20-313(a)	Class 1 misdemeanor (mandatory app.)
20-313.1(a)	Making a false certification concerning financial responsibility	20-313.1(a)	Class 1 misdemeanor (mandatory app.)
20-313.1(b)	Giving false information to DMV concerning another's financial responsibility, knowing or having reason to believe that such information is false	20-313.1(b)	Class 1 misdemeanor (mandatory app.)

Appendix A
1999 Waiver List

UNIFORM POLICIES RELATING TO TRAFFIC OFFENSES

TRAFFIC OFFENSES FOR WHICH COURT APPEARANCE IS MANDATORY

(Adopted by the Conference of Chief District Judges, October 1, 1998 pursuant to N.C. G.S. 7A-148)

Applies To Offenses Committed On Or After January 1, 1999

1. All pleas of **not** guilty.
2. All felonies.
3. Driving while subject to an impairing substance. [G.S. 20-138.1]
4. Driving a commercial vehicle while subject to an impairing substance. [G.S. 20-138.2]
5. Careless and reckless driving. [G.S. 20-140]
6. Exceeding the applicable speed limit by over 15 mph while driving over 55 mph.
7. Driving in excess of 80 mph. [G.S. 20-141]
8. Use of radar detector in commercial vehicle. [19A NCAC 3D .0801 (a), (b); 49CFR 392.71; 20-396]
9. Passing stopped school bus. [G.S. 20-217]
10. Failure to stop for emergency vehicles. [G.S. 20-157(a)]
11. Failure to obey directions of a traffic officer, or of a fireman at the scene of a fire. [G.S. 20-114.1]
12. Failure to stop, etc., at the scene of an accident, or failure to report such an accident. [G.S. 20-166; G.S. 20-166.1]
13. Driving while (license) suspended, revoked or disqualified, or permitting an owned vehicle to be so operated. [G.S. 20-28; G.S. 20-34]
14. Driving a commercial motor vehicle without being licensed to do so, or driving a commercial motor vehicle while license suspended, revoked, or subject to a disqualification or out of service order. [G.S. 20-28(c); G.S. 20-37.12]
15. Possess fictitious, canceled, revoked, suspended or altered license, or counterfeit, sell, lend, or permit use of license by another or any other violation of G.S. 20-30.
16. Any violation of the financial responsibility laws. [Chapter 20, Articles 9A and 13]
17. Any violation of the vehicle registration laws involving stolen or altered registration plates or certificates.
18. Selling handicapped parking placards. [G.S. 20-37.6(c3)]
19. Any violation involving a false affidavit, or false statement under oath, or perjury. [G.S. 20-17(5); G.S. 20-31; G.S. 20-112; G.S. 20-313.1]
20. Any violation charged in the same citation, warrant, magistrate's order, or summons with a mandatory court appearance violation.
21. Death by vehicle. [G.S. 20-141.4]
22. Impaired instruction. [G.S. 20-12.1]
23. Transporting spent nuclear fuel without notifying Highway Patrol. [G.S. 20-167.1]
24. Driving by a person under 21 while drinking or after having consumed alcohol or controlled substance. [G.S. 20-138.3]
25. Racing (prearranged, spontaneous, permitting such use of an owned vehicle, betting on prearranged racing). [G.S. 20-141.3]
26. Unlawful use of red or blue lights on vehicle. [G S. 20-130.1]
27. Failure to give way to the right when being passed. [G.S. 20-149(b)]
28. Driving with open container after drinking. [G.S. 20-138.7]
29. Driving to elude arrest. [G.S. 20-141.5]
30. Operating commercial vehicle after consuming alcohol. [G.S. 20-138.2A]
31. Operating school bus, school activity bus, or child care vehicle after consuming alcohol. [G.S. 20-138.2B]

SOURCE: Administrative Office of the Courts (1998).

TRAFFIC OFFENSES FOR WHICH COURT APPEARANCE MAY BE WAIVED

(on execution of written waiver of appearance and trial, and plea of guilty/responsible)
(Adopted by the Conference of Chief District Judges, October 1, 1998 pursuant to N.C. G.S. 7A-148)

Applies To Offenses Committed On Or Affer January 1, 1999

A. Speeding Violations:

1. Speed over the applicable limit and over 55 mph but not over 80 mph	0–5	6–10	11–15	
Costs plus fine of	$0	$10	$25	
2. Speed over the applicable limit but 55 mph or under	0–5	6–10	11–15	16 & Over
Costs plus fine of	$0	$10	$25	$50

B. Other Violations:

1. Driving without, or with expired non-commercial driver's license (except when revoked or suspended), or operating motorcycle without proper license endorsement, or knowingly permitting an owned vehicle to be so operated .... $50 and Costs
2. Failure to yield right of way to emergency vehicles, except as provided in No. 10 of mandatory appearances. [G.S. 20-156, -157] .... $25 and Costs
3. Failure to use seat belts. [G.S. 20-135.2A] $25
4. Failure to wear helmet, or having too many passengers, on motorcycle or moped. [G.S. 20-140.4] $25
5. Driving the wrong way on a dual-lane highway .... $25 and Costs
6. Improper passing .... $25 and Costs
7. Failure to dim lights .... $10 and Costs
8. Height, length and width violations .... $10 and Costs
9. Failure to use child restraint systems. [G.S. 20-137.1] .... $25 and Costs
10. Driving too slowly .... $5 and Costs
11. Illegal parking in handicapped space $50
12. Any other parking violation .... Costs
13. Violation of vehicle inspection law .... Costs
14. Exceeding a safe speed .... $25 and Costs
15. Following too closely .... $25 and Costs
16. Failure to stop for a red light or stop sign or flashing red light .... $25 and Costs
17. Failure to yield right-of-way .... $25 and Costs
18. Improper turn and/or improper signal .... $10 and Costs
19. Driving the wrong way on a one-way city street .... $25 and Costs
20. Improper vehicle equipment .... Costs
21. Use of darkened windows in motor vehicle. [G.S. 20-127(b)–(d)] .... $50 and Costs
22. Failure to reduce speed to avoid accident .... $25 and Costs
23. Violation of the vehicle registration laws, except as in No. 17 of mandatory appearances .... $25 and Costs
24. Failure to use headlights when wipers on $5
25. Speeding in a work zone. [G.S. 20-141(j2)] .... $150 and Costs
26. Any other traffic violation for which court appearance is not mandatory .... $10 and Costs
27. Littering [under G.S. 14-399(c) only] .... $100 and Costs
28. Operating vehicle with improper dealer plates. [G.S. 20-79(e)(1)] .... $50 and Costs
29. Transporting child under 12 in open bed or open cargo area. [G.S. 20-135.2B] $25
30. Speeding in school zone or on school property. [G.S. 20-141.1, -141(e1)] .... $25 and Costs

OTHER POLICIES RELATING TO TRAFFIC OFFENSES:

1. G.S. 7A-148 provides that the Conference of Chief District Judges shall prepare a "uniform schedule" of waivable traffic offenses and otherwise promote the "uniform administration of justice." In accordance with the statutory mandate, all judicial districts will adhere to the schedule provided herein and individual judicial district policies deviating from this schedule are prohibited.
2. Where more than one charge is made on a uniform traffic citation, the defendant shall be fined only for the offense carrying the highest fine. Only one bill of costs will be assessed.
3. When a defendant is charged with two traffic offenses arising out of the same transaction, only one citation should be used. If an additional one or two offenses arising out of the same transaction are charged, they should be placed on a separate citation.

Source: Administrative Office of the Courts (1998).

Appendix B
North Carolina Motor Vehicle Point System

§ 20-16. Authority of Division to suspend license.

(a) The Division shall have authority to suspend the license of any operator with or without a preliminary hearing upon a showing by its records or other satisfactory evidence that the licensee:

(1) to (4) Repealed by Session Laws 1979, c. 36;

(5) Has, under the provisions of subsection (c) of this section, within a three-year period, accumulated 12 or more points, or eight or more points in the three-year period immediately following the reinstatement of a license which has been suspended or revoked because of a conviction for one or more traffic offenses;

(6) Has made or permitted an unlawful or fraudulent use of such license or a learner's permit, or has displayed or represented as his own, a license or learner's permit not issued to him;

(7) Has committed an offense in another state, which if committed in this State would be grounds for suspension or revocation;

(8) Has been convicted of illegal transportation of alcoholic beverages;

(8a) Has been convicted of impaired instruction under G.S. 20-12.1;

(8b) Has violated on a military installation a regulation of that installation prohibiting conduct substantially equivalent to conduct that constitutes impaired driving under G.S. 20-138.1 and, as a result of that violation, has had his privilege to drive on that installation revoked or suspended after an administrative hearing authorized by the commanding officer of the installation and that commanding officer has general court martial jurisdiction;

(9) Has, within a period of 12 months, been convicted of two or more charges of speeding in excess of 55 and not more than 80 miles per hour, or of one or more charges of reckless driving and one or more charges of speeding in excess of 55 and not more than 80 miles per hour;

(10) Has been convicted of operating a motor vehicle at a speed in excess of 75 miles per hour on a public road or highway where the maximum speed is less than 70 miles per hour;

(10a) Has been convicted of operating a motor vehicle at a speed in excess of 80 miles per hour on a public highway where the maximum speed is 70 miles per hour; or

(11) Has been sentenced by a court of record and all or a part of the sentence has been suspended and a condition of suspension of the sentence is that the operator not operate a motor vehicle for a period of time.

However, if the Division revokes without a preliminary hearing and the person whose license is being revoked requests a hearing before the effective date of the revocation, the licensee retains his license unless it is revoked under some other provision of the law, until the hearing is held, the person withdraws his request, or he fails to appear at a scheduled hearing.

(b) Pending an appeal from a conviction of any violation of the motor vehicle laws of this State, no driver's license shall be suspended by the Division of Motor Vehicles because of such conviction or because of evidence of the commission of the offense for which the conviction has been had.

(c) The Division shall maintain a record of convictions of every person licensed or required to be licensed under the provisions of this Article as an operator and shall enter therein records of all convictions of such persons for any violation of the motor vehicle laws of this State and shall assign to the record of such person, as of the date of commission of the offense, a number of points for every such conviction in accordance with the following schedule of convictions and points, except that points shall not be assessed for convictions resulting in suspensions or revocations under other provisions of laws: Further, any points heretofore charged for violation of the motor vehicle inspection laws shall not be considered by the Division of Motor Vehicles as a basis for suspension or revocation of driver's license:

Schedule of Point Values

Passing stopped school bus	5
Reckless driving	4
Hit and run, property damage only	4
Following too close	4
Driving on wrong side of road	4
Illegal passing	4
Running through stop sign	3
Speeding in excess of 55 miles per hour	3
Failing to yield right-of-way	3
Running through red light	3
No driver's license or license expired more than one year	3
Failure to stop for siren	3
Driving through safety zone	3
No liability insurance	3
Failure to report accident where such report is required	3
Speeding in a school zone in excess of the posted school zone speed limit	3
All other moving violations	2
Littering pursuant to G.S. 14-399 when the littering involves the use of a motor vehicle	1

The above provisions of this subsection shall only apply to violations and convictions which take place within the State of North Carolina.

No points shall be assessed for conviction of the following offenses:

Overloads
Over length
Over width
Over height
Illegal parking
Carrying concealed weapon
Improper plates
Improper registration
Improper muffler
Public drunk within a vehicle
Possession of alcoholic beverages
Improper display of license plates or dealers' tags
Unlawful display of emblems and insignia
Failure to display current inspection certificate.

In case of the conviction of a licensee of two or more traffic offenses committed on a single occasion, such licensee shall be assessed points for one offense only and if the offenses involved have a different point value, such licensee shall be assessed for the offense having the greater point value.

Upon the restoration of the license or driving privilege of such person whose license or driving privilege has been suspended or revoked because of conviction for a traffic offense, any points that might previously have been accumulated in the driver's record shall be cancelled.

Whenever any licensee accumulates as many as seven points or accumulates as many as four points during a three-year period immediately following reinstatement of his license after a period of suspension or revocation, the Division may request the licensee to attend a conference regarding such licensee's driving record. The Division may also afford any licensee who has accumulated as many as seven points or any licensee who has accumulated as many as four points within a three-year period immediately following reinstatement of his license after a period of suspension or revocation an opportunity to attend a driver improvement clinic operated by the Division and, upon the successful completion of the course taken at the clinic, three points shall be deducted from the licensee's conviction record; provided, that only one deduction of points shall be made on behalf of any licensee within any five-year period.

When a license is suspended under the point system provided for herein, the first such suspension shall be for not more than 60 days; the second such suspension shall not exceed six months and any subsequent suspension shall not exceed one year.

Whenever the driver's license of any person is subject to suspension under this subsection and at the same time also subject to suspension or revocation under other provisions of laws, such suspensions or revocations shall run concurrently.

In the discretion of the Division, a period of probation not to exceed one year may be substituted for suspension or for any unexpired period of suspension under subsections (a)(1) through (a)(10a) of this section. Any violation of probation during the probation period shall result in a suspension for the unexpired remainder of the suspension period. Any accumulation of three or more points under this subsection during a period of probation shall constitute a violation of the condition of probation.

(d) Upon suspending the license of any person as authorized in this section, the Division shall immediately notify the licensee in writing and upon his request shall afford him an opportunity for a hearing, unless a preliminary hearing was held before his license was suspended, as early as practical within not to exceed 30 days after receipt of such request. The hearing shall be conducted in the district court district as defined in G.S. 7A-133 wherein the licensee resides. Hearings shall be rotated among all the counties within that district if the district contains more than one county unless the Division and the licensee agree that such hearing may be held in some other district, and such notice shall contain the provisions of this section printed thereon. Upon such hearing the duly authorized agents of the Division may administer oaths and may issue subpoenas for the attendance of witnesses and the production of relevant books and papers and may require a reexamination of the licensee. Upon such hearing the Division shall either rescind its order of suspension, or good cause appearing therefor, and may extend the suspension of such license. Provided further upon such hearing, preliminary or otherwise, involving subsections (a)(1) through (a)(10a) of this section, the Division may for good cause appearing in its discretion substitute a period of probation not to exceed one year for the suspension or for any unexpired period of suspension. Probation shall mean any written agreement between the suspended driver and a duly authorized representative of the Division and such period of probation shall not exceed one year, and any violation of the probation agreement during the probation period shall result in a suspension for the unexpired remainder of the suspension period. The authorized agents of the Division shall have the same powers in connection with a preliminary hearing prior to suspension as this subsection provided in connection with hearings held after suspension. These agents shall also have the authority to take possession of a surrendered license on behalf of the Division if the suspension is upheld and the licensee requests that the suspension begin immediately.

(e) The Division may conduct driver improvement clinics for the benefit of those who have been convicted of one or more violations of this Chapter. Each driver attending a driver improvement clinic shall pay a fee of twenty-five dollars ($25.00).

(e1) Notwithstanding any other provision of this Chapter, if the Division suspends the license of an operator pursuant to subdivisions (a)(9), (a)(10), or (a)(10a) of this section, upon the first suspension only, a district court judge may allow the licensee a limited driving privilege or license for a period not to exceed 12 months, provided he has not been convicted of any other motor vehicle moving violation within the previous 12 months. The limited driving privilege shall be issued in the same manner and under the terms and conditions prescribed in G.S. 20-16.1(b)(1), (2), (3), (4), and (5).

Index to Punishment Chart for North Carolina Motor Vehicle Offenses

Major offenses are listed in alphabetical order, showing the section number for each.